The Queen's Frog Prince

The courtship of Elizabeth I and the Duke of Anjou

The Queen's Frog Prince

The courtship of Elizabeth I and the Duke of Anjou

David Lee

Winchester, UK
Washington, USA

JOHN HUNT PUBLISHING

First published by Chronos Books, 2023
Chronos Books is an imprint of John Hunt Publishing Ltd., No. 3 East St., Alresford,
Hampshire SO24 9EE, UK
office@jhpbooks.com
www.johnhuntpublishing.com
www.chronosbooks.com

For distributor details and how to order please visit the 'Ordering' section on our website.

ISBN: 978 1 80341 164 4
978 1 80341 165 1 (ebook)
Library of Congress Control Number: 2022938589

A CIP catalogue record for this book is available from the British Library.

Design: Matthew Greenfield

UK: Printed and bound by CPI Group (UK) Ltd, Croydon, CR0 4YY
Printed in North America by CPI GPS partners

We operate a distinctive and ethical publishing philosophy in
all areas of our business, from our global network of authors to
production and worldwide distribution.

Contents

For my cousin Susan, who taught me that if I could tell a good story, the world would listen.

Tangled was I in Love's snare.
Oppressed with pain, torment with care;
Of grief right sure, of joy quite bare,
Clean in despair by cruelty.

–Thomas Wyatt

Illustrations

1. Elizabeth I coronation miniature by Nicholas Hilliard c. 1600 after a lost original of c. 1559. (Wikimedia Commons).
2. Young Elizabeth I portrait, attributed to William Scrots (c. 1546) (Via Wikimedia Commons).
3. A portrait of Queen Katherine Parr (1512–1548), sixth and last wife of Henry VIII of England attributed to Master John (c. 1600). Formerly thought to be Lady Jane Grey. (Via Wikimedia Commons).
4. Thomas Seymour, 1st Baron Seymour of Sudeley, by Nicholas Denisot (c. 1547-1549). (Via Wikimedia Commons).
5. William Cecil, Lord Burghley, Attributed to the Workshop of Marcus Gheeraerts the Younger, c. 1580s. (Wikimedia Commons).
6. Robert Dudley, 1st Earl of Leicester, by an unknown artist (c. 1575) (Via Wikimedia Commons).
7. Lettice Knollys, Countess of Essex and Leicester, attributed to George Gower (c. 1585) (Via Wikimedia Commons).
8. Prince Hercule-François, Duke of Alençon, later Duke of Anjou, by an unknown artist, (c. 1572) (Via Wikimedia Commons).
9. Catherine de' Medici and her children, by François Clouet, (1561) (Via Wikimedia Commons).
10. Portrait of Elizabeth I of England Westminster school, by an unknown artist (c. 1580) (Via Wikimedia Commons).

Foreword by Sandra Vasoli

Gloriana—England's Virgin Queen: compelling, resolute, imperious. History revels in her legend, firing endless conjecture about Elizabeth I, the queen and the woman. Elizabeth lore is ever-present; her courageous image is conveyed in myriad ways by artists, historians, authors, actors.

However, this profile—*The Queen's Frog Prince*—is beautifully unique. To read and savor it is to experience the conflicts of life Elizabeth endured.

Author David Lee has accomplished an exceptional feat. It seems he has inhabited the psyche of Elizabeth, and with sensitivity and perception, he has portrayed her as the woman who longed to love and be loved in return. And as I turned page after page, immersed, I became increasingly attuned to Elizabeth's internal struggle to justify her noble duty to rule England with the female yearning to be a lover, wife, mother.

I have had the privilege of knowing David long enough to be amazed at his keen judgment— notably regarding historical figures. He has an extraordinary ability to read between the lines of documents and archival records and capture the very human traits common to us all. With this understanding, a capacity to write delightful prose, and an undeniable wit and sense of humor, he's created a book that is an absolute joy.

Lee's descriptions of Elizabeth shape an entirely different perspective from the genderless, iconic virginal goddess which the Tudor propaganda machine created and history has recited. Instead, dear reader, you will experience Elizabeth—from her early years—as an intensely emotional being, one who regularly formed deep attachments to those close to her. He clarifies that, at times, these needful relationships were the source of great disappointment and pain to Elizabeth. She craved love, and Lee's superbly composed and written narrative reveals that longing as a driving force throughout Elizabeth's life.

The author adeptly addresses the male relationships Elizabeth fostered. In a particularly poignant statement about her affiliation with the Duke of Anjou, he claims "Many princes and gentlemen pursued her, and the hunt for her hand was probably one of history's greatest tragedies of the heart. In the end, the man she wished to marry, who also wished to marry her, would be denied to her."

As for her almost lifelong entanglement with Robert Dudley, Earl of Leicester, Lee does a skillful job of steering the reader through its turbulent ups and downs; the dramas often causing Elizabeth great anguish. Her enduring but unrequited love for him was dashed once and for all when he betrayed her by marrying Lettice Knollys—unbeknownst to Elizabeth. As Lee describes the longings of a woman whose beauty and desirability are fading, he presents the emergence of a new and perhaps unanticipated liaison in the aging queen's life with Francis, Duke of Anjou. Descriptively, he weaves the tale of their unusual friendship and courtship, and I found the fascinating account of their eventual meeting and the resulting bond to be a highlight. The reader can grasp, with empathy, the attraction between a young man with physical imperfections and an older woman whose absolute power doesn't fulfill the need to be cherished and desired.

This unique attachment with the Duke ultimately failed to convince Elizabeth to pursue her desires and abandon the obligation of her birthright, although it came closer to consummation than any of her other loves. David Lee draws us into Elizabeth's private pain: wooing and being wooed by men she adored, only to remain single, celibate, and childless.

Lee provides us with a bittersweet quote from Elizabeth I as her life approached its end, emblematic of the path she ultimately chose: "...all my husbands, my good people."

David Lee has done the memory of Elizabeth Tudor—Queen

Elizabeth I—a great service. He's shared with us, his readers, details of the touching devotion between the queen and her beloved 'Frog,' and in doing so, we gain a rare and intimate glimpse of the vulnerable woman behind the elaborately constructed veil: that grand and queenly image which comes to mind whenever we hear her name.

– Sandra Vasoli

Acknowledgements

I would like to thank the following people who have played a pivotal role in assisting me to complete this book.

Firstly, my husband Victor, who encouraged me from the very beginning to sit down and write. Your belief in me is astounding, and I am forever grateful for your support, and lucky to call you my husband.

My parents, Mary and David, and my brother Conor for their continued support and belief in me.

My close friends and fellow historians, Mary Clancy-Brown and Sandra Vasoli, who continuously encouraged and supported me throughout this process. Your kindness and friendship means so much to me. Particular thanks to Sandra Vasoli for writing the foreword for this book.

My first editor, Eamon Ó Cléirigh, who guided me through the toughest parts of writing and editing this book. Your honesty, encouragement and dedication makes this work a product of your immense talent as much as it is of my passion.

Professor Terence Dooley, Dr Dympna Mc Loughlin, Dr Laura Brown, Professor Marian Lyons and Dr Jennifer Redmond of Maynooth University for each nurturing my passion for history in their own unique way.

My copy-editor Sarah-Beth Watkins, and all from John Hunt Publishing, who have contributed to making my dreams a reality, and the final product of this work absolutely impeccable.

Dramatis Personae

Throughout Elizabeth I's life, a number of fascinating and influential figures experienced what it was like not only to be in the presence of the queen but to also be favoured by her. The chance to become a favourite of England's Virgin Queen often depended on one's position in society or at court, the impression one made on the queen, or simply her mood. She had many favourites, both men and women, and some were given nicknames, often derogatory in nature. Below is a short biographical list of some of her favourites, along with any given nickname where appropriate.

Ashley, Katherine (c.1502 – 1565)

Katherine Ashley (née Champernowne), known affectionately to the queen as 'Kat', was Elizabeth's governess, Lady of the Bedchamber, and close friend and confidante from July 1536 until her death in 1565. In 1545, she married John Ashley, who was Elizabeth's Gentleman attendant and Anne Boleyn's cousin. John would later become Master of the Jewel House upon Elizabeth's ascension. Kat witnessed Elizabeth's fall from grace, restoration to the succession, abuses at the hands of Thomas Seymour, and the succession of all three of Henry VIII's children. Ever the loyal friend and servant to her mistress, she spent some time at Fleet Prison during Elizabeth's imprisonment at the Tower of London and later house arrest at Hatfield, during the reign of Mary I. She was given the highest-ranking female position as Lady of the Bedchamber when Elizabeth finally succeeded in 1558. In 1565, she died suddenly yet peacefully in her early sixties, away from court, and would never witness the queen's courtship with Anjou. Her death brought much distress to Elizabeth, who wished she had been by her friend's side at the end. Kat was succeeded as Chief Gentlewoman of the Privy Chamber by Blanche Parry.

Cecil, William (1520 – 1598)

William Cecil was a statesman and Chief Adviser of Elizabeth I from the beginning of her reign in 1558 until his death in 1598. He is referred to as 'Burghley' in this book, as he was later entitled 1st Baron Burghley in 1571. Cecil was given the nickname 'Spirit' by Elizabeth and held many high and official positions during her reign, such as Secretary of State, Leader of the Privy Council, Lord Privy Seal, and Lord High Treasurer. His grandfather, David Cecil, was a favourite Yeoman of Henry VII, Elizabeth's grandfather and first Tudor Monarch. Burghley was the cousin of one of her favourite ladies, Blanche Parry, and had served as an administrator in her household when she was a princess. Like Elizabeth, Burghley was a Protestant and suffered somewhat during the reign of Mary I. He urged his queen to marry during her early reign, to little avail. Later, he would support her endeavour to marry Anjou. He married twice, first to Mary Cheke, who died in 1543, then later to Mildred Cooke, who died in 1589. Burghley had many children, notably Thomas Cecil, who would become 1st Earl of Exeter; Anne Cecil, who became Countess of Oxford by marriage; and Robert Cecil, who became 1st Earl of Salisbury and, later, successor to his father's position as Lord High Treasurer. It is said that, as Burghley lay on his deathbed, Queen Elizabeth fed him soup with her own hand.

Cecil, Robert (1563 – 1612)

Robert was the younger son of William Cecil. His mother was Mildred Cooke, Lord Burghley's second wife. Robert was short, even for the period, and suffered from scoliosis, which gave him a hunchback. For his deformity, he endured much ridicule at the hands of courtiers and the public. He was intensely disliked, in general, unlike his father, who was popular amongst the Elizabethan court. As a result of his physical appearance, Elizabeth affectionately referred to him as her 'Pygmy', which wasn't then deemed a derogatory term. King James I would also refer to him as 'my little beagle'. Despite his malformation, he had a successful career as a Privy Councilor, Chancellor of the Duchy of Lancaster, and a leading minister and Secretary of State upon the death of his father in 1598. He married Elizabeth Brooke and they had two children. The queen greatly admired him and revered him for his intelligence. He would be responsible for organizing the secret succession of James VI of Scotland as the queen's heir long before it became apparent that she was dying. Despite this, he greatly mourned Elizabeth's death. Over the years, he had an ongoing rivalry with Robert Devereux, 2nd Earl of Essex and favourite of the queen. Cecil died in 1612, apparently from cancer. His tomb can be found in Hatfield Parish Church.

de Simier, Jean

Little is known about the personal life of Simier, who was a close friend of the Duke of Anjou. However, he was a servant to and ambassador for the duke and so must have come from a somewhat agreeable background. He was sent to woo Elizabeth in December of 1578, amidst the marriage negotiations. This was Anjou's way of making sure he would be conveyed in a manner which Elizabeth would find attractive, even seductive. Simier was the best person for this job and his attempts to woo the queen were successful, though whether the queen was initially interested in Simier rather than the duke is open to speculation. Simier's words were an attempt to 'make love' to the queen by proxy. In many ways, his presence would have piqued her curiosity and desire to meet Anjou in person. Elizabeth favoured Simier, stating that he was 'sage and discreet beyond his years...'. Simier wasn't so popular amongst the English court, who mostly opposed the Anglo-French marriage negotiations. She fondly referred to him as her 'Monkey'. It was her 'Monkey' who would soon have her hooked on the idea of wedding her 'Frog' prince.

Devereux, Robert (1565 – 1601)

Robert Devereux was the son of Lettice Knollys and Walter Devereux, 1st Earl of Essex. He became the 2nd Earl of Essex upon his father's death. His mother married Lord Robert Dudley, Earl of Leicester, favourite and rumoured lover of Queen Elizabeth. Devereux would marry Frances Walsingham, daughter of Sir Francis Walsingham (Elizabeth's Spymaster) and, ironically, the widow of Sir Philip Sidney, who once opposed Elizabeth's endeavour to marry the Duke of Anjou. They would have two children, one of whom would marry into the Seymour family, becoming the Duchess of Somerset. Essex was a favourite of Elizabeth, yet his frustration with and underestimation of her would eventually cost him his life. He often behaved badly towards her, and his lack of respect earned him many enemies at court, one being Robert Cecil, 2nd Baron Burghley. At one stage, he became a member of the Privy Council, and even played a part in defeating the Armada in 1589, going on to be made Lord Lieutenant of Ireland. However, his veiled threats and eventual open rebellion against the queen and her government in early 1601 was his undoing. He was beheaded on 25th February of that year at Tower Green, the Tower of London, being the last person to face execution there in such a manner. His son, also named Robert, became the 3rd Earl of Essex and was also a royal favourite, as one of James I's 'special friends'.

Duke of Anjou, Francis (1555 – 1584)

Francis, referred to as 'the Duke of Anjou', 'the duke' or simply 'Anjou' in this book. The youngest son of King Henry II of France and Catherine de' Medici. Given the name Hercule at birth, Anjou was twice proposed as a possible match for Elizabeth I of England, though the first proposed negotiations were rejected due to his young age. Later on, Elizabeth would take up negotiations of marriage again, which led to a long and complicated courtship that would end in regret. Francis was scarred from the age of eight or nine due to smallpox. Though he survived this ailment, he would often be ridiculed due to his pockmarked face. He suffered from a slightly deformed spine, which meant that his given name did not suit.

Anjou later changed his name to Francis in honour of his late brother, Francis II of France. He was made heir presumptive to the French throne in 1574 upon the ascension of his brother, Henry III of France, and given the title of Duke of Anjou in 1576. Despite the age gap between him and Elizabeth, the two got on very well and he visited her at the English court twice. They wrote many letters to one another and some of her poems are based on her courtship with him. She affectionately referred to him as her 'Frog', a nickname he did not seem to mind. Their courtship has often been overlooked as a mere political alliance of convenience, and while they wished to marry, by 1580, it was apparent that due to religious complexities, it was impossible. Anjou was awarded the Duchy of Anjou and 'Protector of the Liberty of the Netherlands', yet was unpopular due to his many failed military campaigns. He died of Malaria in 1584 at the age of 29. His death was deeply mourned by Elizabeth, who carried a miniature of him around her waist for the rest of her life.

Dudley, Robert (1532 – 1588)

Robert Dudley, Earl of Leicester, affectionately known as 'Eyes', 'Sweet Robin', or 'Rob' by Queen Elizabeth, and referred to in this book as 'Dudley', was born to the traitor Duke of Northumberland (who attempted to put Jane Grey on the throne instead of Mary I) and Jane Guildford. Dudley's paternal grandfather, Edmund Dudley, was an adviser to Henry VII. It is unknown when he first came into contact with Elizabeth but he became her close confidante and most favourite courtier, rising to great power when she succeeded to the throne. He first married Amy Robsart in 1550, in the presence of King Edward VI. Some say it was a love match, yet, with the ascension of Elizabeth in 1558, he paid little attention to his wife and she remained isolated, away from court and out of the queen's sight. Rumour had it that he was simply waiting for his wife to die so he could marry the queen. In 1560, Amy died, yet, due to suspicious circumstances of her death and talk of Elizabeth and Dudley's involvement, any chance he had of marrying her was gone. He later secretly married Lettice Knollys, one of Elizabeth's ladies and her kin through Boleyn descent. This secret marriage enraged the queen, leading to Dudley being banished from her presence for a time. He later gained favour again but Lettice was never welcomed back to court. Dudley overtly opposed the Anjou match, yet his pleas fell on deaf ears. His death in 1588 devastated Elizabeth, and she kept his last letter, dated six days before his passing, until her own demise in 1603, fifteen years later.

Hatton, Christopher (1540 – 1591)

Sir Christopher Hatton was an English politician, Lord Chancellor of England, and a favourite courtier of Elizabeth's after attracting her attention in 1561. Handsome and skilled, his dancing soon won him her favour and she nicknamed him 'The Dancing Chancellor'. He apparently fell madly in love with her, yet his unusual manner often left her uncomfortable and she could never decide whether she truly liked him or not. Nonetheless, he had a successful career and position at court and even travelled with Francis Drake on occasion. He was opposed to the marriage negotiations between Elizabeth and the Duke of Anjou, and her openness regarding her affections for the duke left him on the verge of tears. While he wrote often of his love for her, his attempts to woo her were never taken seriously. He built a lavish mansion in Northamptonshire, as big as Hampton Court, called Holdenby House, which almost bankrupted him. His health declined and he died in 1591 at Ely Palace.

Knollys, Lettice (1543 – 1634)

Lettice Knollys was introduced to court early in life. When her mother, Katherine Knollys (née Carey), became a senior Lady of the Bedchamber after the succession of Elizabeth. Lettice was also given a position as a Maid of the Privy Chamber. Her mother was the daughter of Mary Boleyn and William Carey, and thus the Knollys ladies and the queen shared Boleyn blood. Many historians state that Katherine was the daughter of Henry VIII, from his affair with Mary Boleyn in the 1520s. If this were true, Elizabeth and Katherine would not only have been cousins through their maternity, but half-sisters because of their shared paternity. This would also make Elizabeth I Lettice Knollys' aunt. Elizabeth greatly favoured her mother's side of the family, bestowing gifts and appointing them with high positions at court. Lettice first married Walter Devereux, with whom she had four children. One of these was Robert Devereux, 2nd Earl of Essex, who would one day become the queen's favourite but would eventually be executed for charges of treason. In 1578, Lettice married Robert Dudley, Elizabeth's one-time favourite, and rumoured lover. This changed the pair's relationship forever and Lettice was banished from court, never to return. These events may well have encouraged Elizabeth regarding her courtship with the Duke of Anjou. Lettice married once more and lived a life of splendour and luxury up to the old age of 91, almost unheard of for the period.

Parr, Katherine (1512 – 1548)

Katherine Parr was the last of the six wives of King Henry VIII and stepmother to Elizabeth I, Mary I, and Edward VI. She married four times, lastly to Thomas Seymour, 1st Baron Seymour of Sudeley, just months after Henry VIII died, with their marriage having to remain a secret for some time. Katherine brought the Princess Elizabeth to live with her and her new husband in Chelsea. During this time, Seymour began to abuse the princess, and Katherine even assisted her husband during one episode of 'horseplay'. However, soon after Katherine became pregnant, she sent Elizabeth away, likely to save their reputations. The princess would never see her stepmother again, as Katherine died on 5th September, 1548, shortly after giving birth to a baby girl. Notably, Katherine was the first English woman to publish two books in her own name.

Walsingham, Francis (1532 – 1590)

Sir Francis Walsingham was Principal Secretary or Secretary of State and a favourite of Elizabeth's. He worked tirelessly with Lord Burghley for the protection of the queen, national security, and the preservation of the Protestant religion. He is fondly remembered as Elizabeth's 'Spymaster' and is a prime example of a man rising from obscurity to great wealth, power, and influence over the Elizabethan State. Walsingham oversaw the operations that would lead to the execution of Elizabeth's cousin and rival for the English throne, Mary Stuart, Queen of Scots. Like Elizabeth, Walsingham grew up during a time of turmoil in England, where queens were executed and monasteries were dissolved. He shared her vision for England and sought to protect her from harm in relation to foreign policy. While he was instructed to go to France to negotiate a treaty based on discussion around the marriage between Elizabeth and the Duke of Anjou, he opposed the proposed match, most likely fearing an influx of Catholics to the English court if the queen were to marry a foreign, Catholic prince. Despite his blunt opinions, Elizabeth greatly valued his advice, referring to him as her 'Moor', who could not change his colour.

Introduction

The Rising Sun

Elizabeth I has become one of the most recognizable and relatable female historical figures of all time. She has inspired many books, both fictional and academic, as well as numerous theatrical and cinematic portrayals of her dramatic life and reign, not least by William Shakespeare, England's most famous playwright. Quite often, she is referred to as a paradox and still ignites the imaginations of millions across the globe. It can be said that she has come to represent a form of British national identity. Even during her own lifetime, she inspired a new form of courtly etiquette, which became known as the Elizabethan cult of courtly love.

From the beginning of her life in September 1533, her destiny was outlined, with the probable assumption that this little princess would one day play the part of a political pawn to suit some foreign alliance. Though her father, Henry VIII, endeavoured to move heaven and earth to marry her mother, Anne Boleyn, it would have been inconceivable to him that his daughter might one day rule England into a 'Golden age'. Nor could he have suspected upon her birth that she would be the last Tudor monarch to sit on the throne of England. Having spent several years attempting to divorce his first wife, Catherine of Aragon, daughter of Ferdinand of Aragon and Isabella of Castile, he'd hoped that his second marriage to Lady Anne Boleyn, once lady-in-waiting to Catherine, would produce a healthy male heir to secure the Tudor dynasty.

Elizabeth's mother would face an end so violent and unjust, it still inspires academic studies, novels, blogs, websites, movies, and television dramas and documentaries. Her story ran parallel with her daughter's, who would have been too young to remember her or when she was executed. Many believe that Anne's courage was passed down to Elizabeth and remained with her throughout her life and reign. Anne made a dangerous enemy in Thomas Cromwell, Henry's Chief Minister, and her failure to provide England with a male heir, like her predecessor Catherine, did not help her cause.

It is now known that Anne's demise was not only orchestrated by Cromwell but by her own husband, the King. While Elizabeth was her only surviving child, she is believed to have had several pregnancies, miscarriages, and stillbirths. Her daughter's first three years of life were that of a noble, serene princess, who had every want and need fulfilled. By the time of her mother's death, she had her own household, with the belief that she would one day marry a foreign prince, even become a queen-consort herself. It was hoped that her birth might be followed by a boy but, to Anne Boleyn's dismay, no miracle prince would come to save her and her daughter. On 19th May 1536, only three years into her tenure as queen, she was executed within the walls of the Tower of London, based on trumped-up charges of adultery, incest, and treason. Her story has inspired several leading historians to proclaim her innocence, with many observers deeming it highly unlikely that she committed any of these crimes.

We know how her story goes, and her truth has been revealed centuries after her death – her innocence clear, her piety and charitable personality restored, and her position as Henry's loyal wife proclaimed true and valid. So many love the story of Anne Boleyn, just as we love the story of her daughter, who fought hard to survive and who would one day secure the throne of England for herself. Her younger brother, Edward VI, the son of Henry's third wife – Anne's rival – Jane Seymour, would become king at the age of only nine upon his father's death in 1547. He would die young, without issue, in 1553, and would attempt to contradict his father's will, which stated that the order of succession was to be first Edward, then, if he died without issue, Mary, and, if she died without issue, Elizabeth. Edward attempted to place Lady Jane Grey as his heir apparent, due to her staunch Protestantism, which was contrary to that of Mary's devout Catholicism. Jane Grey was the great-granddaughter of Henry VII, through his daughter, Princess Mary Tudor, but she would only reign for nine days. Mary I stamped out Jane's encouraged and pretended claim to the throne and was proclaimed Queen of England on 19th July 1553. Mary and Elizabeth struggled to find a middle ground where religion was concerned.

Both had suffered during their childhood, often subject to their father's changing moods. Elizabeth would suffer not only her father's disfavour and the disgrace of her mother's downfall but also at the hands of her stepfather, Thomas Seymour, 1st Baron Seymour of Sudeley, and fourth husband of her stepmother Katherine Parr, Henry VIII's sixth and final wife. He is suspected of molesting her during her stay with the newly married couple after the death of her father.

She also had to tolerate her sister's ire, and was even imprisoned and questioned due to the Wyatt Plot, which favoured her over Mary. Though both sisters found it difficult to have an amiable relationship due to the many conspiracies to place the Protestant Elizabeth on the throne, she was eventually proclaimed as Mary's successor upon the queen's death in 1558, contradicting all of her father's hopes, her brother's preferences, and her sister's wrath. She would become Gloriana, England's 'Virgin Queen'. Yet, there is another side to Elizabeth that is still to be fully examined; the emotional state of this iconic woman has yet to be interpreted on a larger scale. Who was she underneath the crown, the lead make-up, and the mask of monarchy? What of her relationship with Lord Robert Dudley? And her courtship with her final suitor, the Duke of Anjou? Was Gloriana more complicated than has been perceived for so long? Did she find love, only to be discouraged and let down by those closest to her? Was she the pragmatist so many historians say she was? Or is there more to the woman behind the virgin?

My interest in Elizabeth came about at quite a young age. I was attracted to the story of her mother's downfall, and this interest in the history of Tudor women has stayed with me to the present day. Indeed, I find 'Herstory' a far more appropriate application to the work I do, and in how I see the role of Tudor women in European and World history. In 2018, whilst researching for my undergraduate thesis based on Anne's Boleyn's downfall, I came across the story of Elizabeth's courtship with the Duke of Anjou. At this time, I had little motivation to read too deeply into her love letters to him but made a mental note to come back to them. When I finally submitted my undergraduate dissertation, which was met with much-needed encouragement, I decided to embark on a Master's degree, yet chose to veer away from sixteenth-century women's history in favour of something based on Irish/British nineteenth-century gender history. This is due to my interest in the study of how women of the industrial period identified themselves in society. Though this took up much of my time in terms of research and writing, the beginnings of 2020 brought a welcome opportunity to look into other topics of interest, which led me back to Elizabeth and Anjou. The lockdown of summer 2020 allowed me the time to gather further information based on this oft-overlooked courtship. When I dug deep, I found, to my surprise, that their love letters seem genuine in their display of affection.

Elizabeth has always been identified as a shrewd ruler, who was well versed in the art of foreign-diplomatic alliance. Before reading the letters, I had the impression that she was something of a stone-hearted figure, concerned with her own personal power, and totally opposed to the idea of sharing this with a man. What I found, due to her correspondence with Anjou and her poetry, was a love story so ill-fated and sad that there is no need for a fictional or satirical interpretation. As I looked further in terms of popular works and cinematic adaptations, I discovered that the general view of the Anjou match was overwhelmingly a-historical and contradictory. I was also surprised to find that many historians have either ignored or completely denied any notion of romance or love between the two. What has formed instead is a historiography that suits the narrative of so many historians and novelists. What they fail to see is that her story, when stripped of the propaganda that she herself designed, reveals a woman with true conviction, dedicated to her position as queen, ordained by God, yet ultimately denied the ability to follow her heart as Elizabeth Tudor, rather than Elizabeth Regina. The inherited version of her that we know today, is widely accepted due to her unusual circumstances as queen. Her story fascinates, and her piety and virtue are undisputed. Whether this is because it makes her a mark of national identity or simply more interesting is of little matter. It seems likely that the image we have of her, for all her might, power, and glory, is only half the story. To gain a full insight into the mind of one of England's greatest rulers, we have to challenge our own inherited portrayal of 'Gloriana'.

Elizabeth's reign was triumphant, yet the truth behind her letters to the Duke of Anjou reveal more layers to this iconic story. It may make some historians and authors uncomfortable but the evidence can't be denied. Whether she really fell in love with Anjou, or whether she simply thought she did, has been the entire focus of this work. Though it presents some complicated possibilities that are still in need of further analysis, such as her virginity and her early relationship with Robert Dudley, the aim of this interpretation is by no means an attempt to dismiss her glory. On the contrary, I feel that this narrative can only add to the discussion. The general way in which we remember Elizabeth I and identify her may well have been to her liking but it is not the duty of the historian to portray historical figures the way they wished to be seen, nor how we wish to see them. Therefore, it would be too easy to assume that she instantly fell head over heels in love with Anjou, just as it is too easy to assume that she was totally opposed to marriage or childbearing, or was in love with Robert Dudley.

The reality behind Elizabeth's psychological and emotional state regarding marriage and pregnancy must be considered. I have attempted to reconstruct her emotional state on a number of occasions based on the contents of her letters to Anjou and other members of her court and council. Her relationships with Dudley and Seymour are also paramount in terms of understanding her later decisions to pursue a courtship with Anjou and finally deny herself her desire for him. Elizabeth's sexuality must also be considered, and her emotional distress in relation to a number of important events throughout her life has been taken into account. Though this is only one interpretation of her feelings towards Anjou, I am well aware that it will find opposition. I was surprised to find that so many historians reject the concept of her falling in love with her 'Frog' prince, or at least forming an emotional attachment, in favour of her love of Robert Dudley, who she could never have married anyway.

Many princes and gentlemen pursued her, and the hunt for her hand was probably one of history's greatest tragedies of the heart. In the end, the man she wished to marry, who also wished to marry her, would be denied to her. The duke, though reportedly not the most-handsome man, found a way into the Virgin Queen's affections. This fondness seems to have grown into something more complicated than we could imagine, even considering the amount of contemporary evidence in existence. She was pursued by Austria, Sweden, Spain, and her homeland, England. Yet none would match the charm of France. From the time she was a child, it was assumed that she would marry and that it was her destiny as a woman to do so. Yet, what she accomplished was far greater than could have been imagined. But this doesn't mean that she did not wish to fulfil the obligation of marriage and childbearing. On the contrary, though Elizabeth remained unmarried and probably a virgin, this was only due to the many obstacles in front of her and the duke. Had he been a Protestant, events may well have played out differently.

Like her mother's marriage to Henry VIII and her coronation, her courtship with Anjou was met by the disagreeable, cold, English shoulder. Perhaps her passion for him could have matched that of her father's for Anne Boleyn. Yet, with the example of her father's reign, her mother's fall from grace, and the many traumatic and psychologically damaging events that took place prior to her ascension, it is unsurprising that she chose mind over heart. As the emotional damage from her formative years remained unhealed, right up to the end of her life, it is no surprise that she suffered from nightmares, insomnia, paranoia, and depression. Her unstable childhood and turbulent teenage years would have a profound effect on her early attitude towards marriage and her role as a female ruler. Like no other, she defied sixteenth-century expectations of her gender, and ruled alone. She admired and favoured many, and possibly loved Robert Dudley, but her courtship with Anjou was unique to her reign and life. Never before had she expected to marry and find happiness with a man so many years her junior.

Between 1579 and 1584, Elizabeth's reign would undergo enormous changes, with serious consequences for her mental health. The betrayal of her once-favoured courtier Robert Dudley and her kinswoman Lettice Knollys would propel her on an emotional roller-coaster that ended in tragedy and regret. Yet, it is these events that gave us the Elizabeth we know and recognize today. Without her courtship with the Duke of Anjou, and her falling out with Dudley, she may not have become Gloriana. As it will become clear, her affection for Anjou would have influence over her political decisions, succession complications, and the undesired war with mighty Spain, over which she triumphed. Anjou was present prior to some of her greatest accomplishments and hardest falls, and his influence on her decisions later in life would have an impact like no other on English history.

I could never have imagined how large my interest in their courtship would grow and, as my research developed, I realized the enormity of the task I was about to take on. This is my interpretation of Elizabeth's emotional connection to the Duke of Anjou and is by no means the only narrative I have considered. Yet, the evidence I have consulted dictates that there is more to this courtship than has been previously attested. Again, I was surprised to find that few other historians believe that she loved him, yet I am glad to know that I belong to a minority – not entirely alone in my interpretation. All sources, both primary and secondary, have been carefully selected, and I chose to limit them based on their quality and historical value rather than that of quantity. I have greatly benefitted from online sources from the British Archives and have been lucky enough to find most of Elizabeth's works in printed form, with commentary and analysis for context. The secondary sources I chose to consult are based on my belief in each historian's/author's ability to create a genuine interpretation of events and characters with as little bias as possible. I have full faith in the online documentary sources I consulted, and found that many other historians have also consulted digitized and printed versions of Elizabeth's letters and other works.

Throughout, I modernized the spelling in quotations from original documents and some secondary sources, yet left them in their original state where comprehensible to allow for a more-nuanced interpretation. Most quotations from Elizabeth's letters in French to the Duke of Anjou have already been translated but I made sure to crosscheck translations where necessary. In terms of dates, most are interpreted based on the Gregorian Calendar rather than the Julian Calendar, which England used prior to 1752, yet reference is made to this when required, such as Elizabeth's early letter to the Duke of Anjou in 1579, which is dated as 1580 by modern standards. In terms of language,

I make sure not to reference or judge historical attitudes of modesty, sexuality, medicine, and medical diagnoses by modern standards. However, I make comment on Elizabeth's sexuality and apparent 'molestation' in an attempt to interpret how she may have identified these factors, based on her own writings. I also include a breakdown of many historical figures who appear, based on their origins, position, proximity to, and relationship with the queen, and their role in her courtship with Anjou.

Chapter 1

A Courtly Cult of Love

The tale of this unusual and often overlooked Tudor courtship began in 1579 but her story began much earlier. The English Queen, Elizabeth, was forty-five years old and, perhaps, far beyond the 'game of marriage' she had once played as a young, vivacious monarch. Her suitor, the Duke of Alençon and Anjou, was just twenty-three years old and, by the time of their first meeting in the flesh, Elizabeth had already reigned for over twenty years, and had seen her fair share of suitors. However, from the beginning of her reign, it was clear that she did not share her chief minister Burghley's passion in finding a suitable matrimonial match.

By the time she met Anjou for the first time in person, she had already overcome many battles regarding marriage and the succession with her patriarchal contemporaries, which made up almost the entirety of her council. The reason for Burghley's anxiety regarding her marriage was the belief that no woman could rule alone without the guidance of a husband.[1] His inability to take the queen's side, which often infuriated her, was also due to the fact that, until she married, the succession of the English Crown was in question, as was the future welfare of the realm. It would be Burghley's lifetime ambition during her reign to find her a worthy match in a husband: 'God send Our Mistress a husband and by him a son that we may hope our posterity shall have a masculine succession.'[2]

Elizabeth was under no illusion as to where her duties lay in terms of state affairs and ensuring the safety and prosperity of England. However, if she was to survive this storm, it seems she thought better as to what a marriage – a foreign match – would mean for England. It is possible that she looked to her predecessor and sister, Mary, whose reign lasted only five years and ended disastrously after she unwittingly married her Spanish cousin, Prince Philip of Spain – son of Charles V, Holy Roman Emperor – later to become King of Spain. It is clear that, not only was Mary besotted by Philip, but their marriage, and any production of an heir, would prevent Elizabeth and her Protestant religion from ever ruling England.[3]

Many would use Mary I as an example of why marriage was not only necessary for the succession but to ensure just governance throughout the realm. John Aylmer was a defender of the idea of female monarchy and published his defense in 1559 stating that, though it was acceptable for a woman to rule, disregarding gender, it was inconceivable that she could or would without the guidance of a male co-ruler. It was commonplace for women to be seen as naturally weaker, even feeble and lacking in courage and usefulness. Aylmer was generous in his argument in comparison to some of Elizabeth's male contemporaries. He stated that, while a woman monarch was unusual, it was not unprecedented and did not matter because, though she ruled as sovereign, she was governed herself by the laws of the land and, thus, controlled by the men appointed by her as the judges of these laws.[4]

The subject of gender and ruling often comes into play in many interpretations of Elizabeth's life, reign, and courtships. Some historians of the era would state that she was simply unlucky to live in a period that saw women, royal or otherwise, as subject to the will of men. Others believe that her reign was overtly androgynous, with Elizabeth at the centre of a court willing to acknowledge a woman as ruler but also content to accord her some sort of honorary male status. However, the reality would seem somewhat more complicated than this.[5] While it is true that the Elizabethan period was a male-dominated society, though with an ever-changing psychological view of the role of female power, it is likely that the truth sits somewhere in between. As is ever the case, history can be more complicated, and rarely black and white.

It is often believed that this vision of Elizabeth, as the pale-faced, eternal, virgin queen, played some role in the power that she maintained as a single female ruler. This has been referred to as the 'Cult of Elizabeth', and has been much discussed in terms of the queen's religion. The practice of adorning and almost worshipping her as a demi-goddess-like version of Diana became common practice amongst her male courtiers. By carefully mixing politics with religion and courtly love, she was able to enjoy some sense of the ancient chivalrous pantomime of courtship without having to commit to any suitor in particular, or needing to sleep with any man in general, thus maintaining her virginal status.[6] It would also seem that, despite the grumbling by her contemporaries regarding her gender and refusal to marry, she would use the traditional view to her advantage that women should be subordinate to men and were the weaker sex. When approached or reprimanded by Lord Burghley regarding state affairs that she wished to avoid, the virgin queen would often complain that she was merely a woman.[7]

It was probably, therefore, inconceivable to her male counterparts that her ascension was already much anticipated by her people. Indeed, by the time she came to the throne in 1558 as a young and attractive princess, with Tudor flame-red hair, pasty-white skin, and a wanting presence, it is possible that the English needed some physical referral to past times. The reign of her father, though bloody and long-enduring, brought as much stability to England as it did religious turmoil. Though Henry VIII is now remembered as the man who sent his wives to the execution block just as fast as he found a replacement, it is not the Henry sixteenth-century Englishmen recognized. Due to Elizabeth's ability to promote Tudor propaganda, much like her father and grandfather, it is not surprising that her presence on the throne brought great comfort to many of her people. It is also important to consider that her father's reign, her mother's fall, and her sister's disastrous time in power, were all still in the collective living memory of much of the country and across to the continent.

Mary I is now remembered as 'Bloody Mary' – the first ever English queen to rule in her own right, with a Spanish king at her side, and who burnt hundreds of Protestants in her pursuit to restore Catholicism. Yet for all of her disasters in her short five-year reign, it is clear that she was intent on marrying for the greater good of her country and the succession. Though her marriage would end up an unhappy one, and childless, Mary did fulfil the contemporary role as a queen by marrying. It would end up being her greatest ambition and, yet, her greatest failure. In terms of courtly love and culture, Elizabeth was everything Mary could never have been. Though it seems that there existed amongst her male contemporaries a general unease towards the prospect of having to endure another female ruler, Elizabeth presented somewhat of an alternative example of 'queenship'.

Though she played the part of the meek and feeble woman, it is clear that she intended to govern not only by herself but would de facto be 'the man' that so many wanted her to marry. It could even be argued that she embodied the presence and virility of both a king and queen consort, often referring to herself in masculine terms. This may have been an attempt to fit into a male-dominated world, and it is the belief of many historians that she used her gender to champion her ill-at-ease male counsellors. However, it could also be argued that Elizabeth believed her role as anointed queen, the sole Protestant representative of God in England, was much more about that divinity in itself than her flesh and gender. It is possible that she not only used her virginity, divinity, and gender to her advantage amongst male contemporaries, but that she believed herself to be above any worldly view of the female sex. In other words, in her role as queen and in her divinity, she began as a woman, and became

Gloriana, neither male, nor female, but both.

Her contemporary, Thomas Becon (or Bacon), a clergyman from Norfolk, openly lamented her position as queen and governor of the Church of England: 'Thou has set to rule over us as a woman, whom nature hath formed to be in subjection unto man.'[8] Rather than losing her integrity and sense of divinity when approached with such comments, Elizabeth was secure enough in herself and her position to go along with being 'the exception' to the traditional view towards the role of women and queens. It is also clear that, instead of repressing her existing femininity, she chose to flaunt it. While she may have invented the courtly cult of worship amongst her male courtiers, she inherited her flirtatious attitude and natural understanding of her own sexuality from her mother.[9]

It is perhaps the relationship between Burghley and Elizabeth that provides a clearer appreciation of her battle against his efforts to marry her off. This relationship between councillor and queen may have allowed for a greater understanding of her as a person but also her courtships, and particularly her connection with Anjou – though this would come much later in her life. It is evident that when it came to courtship and the question of her marriage and succession, Burghley was often at the forefront of many heated arguments with his queen. She was stubborn but he was an effective chief secretary and the leader of the Privy Council. It must be mentioned, therefore, that during her reign, despite her amorous close friendship with Lord Robert Dudley, later Earl of Leicester, she chose Burghley wisely, going on to form such trust in him that it is possible he became something of a guiding father-figure to her. Perhaps it is Burghley who became the male figure by her side that she never wanted but ultimately needed. In her first speech at Hatfield on 20th, November 1558, she first addressed Burghley:

...I give you this chardge that you shallbe of my privy counsell and content yourself to take paynes for me and my Realme. This judgement I have of you that you will not be corrupted with any manner of gift, and that you wilbee faithful to the state, and that without respect of my pryvate will you will give me that counsaill that you thinke best, And if you shall knowe any thinge necessarye to bee declared to me of secresye, you shall show it to my self only, and assure yourself I will not fayle to keepe taciturnitye therein, and therefore herewith I chardge you.[10]

It is unclear as to whether Elizabeth was so strongly set against marriage from an early age, although, considering her traumatic childhood and relationship with her sister Mary, it is clear that by the time she came to the throne, she had most likely already made her mind up regarding her role as sovereign and matrimony. It is likely that she lived and died a virgin, as a sexual liaison within the Tudor court would be too difficult a secret to conceal. It is also apparent that, though she reigned alone, she had her favourites, and it is probable that she fell in love on more than one occasion. It would be Elizabeth, herself, who would ponder on love in verse, begging 'let me live with some more sweet content/Or die and so forget what love e'er meant'.[11]

Elizabethan poetry can be interpreted in many ways, and it is common to find multiple meanings and symbols behind carefully chosen words and verses. So, what is the 'sweet content' Elizabeth is referring to here? It is well known that she kept up appearances in terms of marriage with her councillors, always staying one foot ahead. This has often been referred to as 'the marriage game'. Her intentions were clear: to reign alone, if possible for her whole life, while keeping the men around her happy. She had to have known that a suitable and negotiable match could have been found at any time, and that it would be difficult to ward off matrimony forever.[12] This game became a dangerous one, not only because the queen's marriage was a matter of national expectation and political necessity but because she seemed to openly celebrate and flaunt her close relationship with Lord Robert Dudley. Through her own hand, and contemporary accounts of the Elizabethan court, it is clear that she found 'what love meant' in an emotional rather than physical relationship with a man she trusted, and had he not already been married, it is possible she would have considered an English match.

It was often suspected, yet never confirmed, that she and Dudley were lovers, and it is also apparent that on a number of occasions, he was bestowed with honours and luxuries at the expense of the queen, and was sometimes thought to act as a king-in-waiting, if not a king already. It was recorded in the early years of Elizabeth's reign that, upon a particular meeting between her and Dudley in 1566, he, along with a train of several-hundred lords, gentlemen, and knights, entered London. He was followed, not only by his own footmen, which was common, but, interestingly, the queen's footmen were also in tow. Elizabeth is said to have come 'secretly' across London Bridge, with only a couple of her ladies accompanying her. When the pair met, they greeted with kisses before riding away together towards Greenwich Palace.[13] This account was recorded by the antiquarian John Stow, and though it would seem he was an eye-witness to this meeting and the gestures that took place, it does not necessarily mean that this encounter was an intentional display of the rumoured affair between the two. Such gestures of kissing and warm greetings between Elizabeth and her favourites would become almost customary during her reign, and were ultimately a part of the Elizabethan courtly cult of love. It is clear, however, that to suspect a romantic relationship between them based on this account is not without merit, due to the grandeur and ceremony attributed to Dudley's arrival on this occasion.

Sadly, for Elizabeth, yet perhaps luckily for the realm, there would be a constant obstacle between her and the possibility of a match in matrimony with Lord Robert – Amy Robsart, his wife. Dudley had married Amy, daughter of Sir Robert Robsart, Lord of the Manor of Syderstone, in Norfolk on 5th June 1550, some time prior to Elizabeth's ascension. Whether Elizabeth and Robert were romantically involved by this time is unclear, yet they were close companions, and she attended the ceremony as the Lady Elizabeth.[14] By the time she came to the throne, unexpectedly, Dudley's fortunes and favour had risen, though many in court expressed their anger and anxiety at this. He was also entitled and made a Knight of the Garter and Master of the Queen's Horse. This is where Elizabeth's relationship with her favourite was often speculated to be romantic and sexual in nature, due to this position requiring his constant close proximity to the queen on a daily basis.

Though this position would have been welcomed by the ambitious Dudley and his family, such a promotion had dire implications for Amy. This is where rumours began, along with the sad road to Amy's demise. In 1559, the Spanish ambassador to Elizabeth's court, Don Gomez Suarez de Figueroa Feria, wrote to the King of Spain, stating that, 'Lord Robert has come into so much favour that he does whatever he likes with affairs, and it is even said that her Majesty visits him in his chamber day and night. People talk so freely that they go so far as to say that his wife has a malady in one of her breasts and the Queen is only waiting for her to die to marry Lord Robert.'[15]

Feria also suggested to King Philip that he approach Dudley on his behalf to promise him 'help and favour'. However, this must have seemed unwise to Philip as the suggestion went no further and Feria returned to Spain shortly after his encounter and report to the king. Philip probably had good reason for avoiding Dudley in terms of alliance, possibly because he was unpredictable, and the queen's council were often suspicious of his informality with her and distrusted him in general. Burghley particularly disfavoured Elizabeth's friendship with him, and was infuriated by his unprecedented closeness to her. It is unsurprising, therefore, that his disapproval of Dudley led to conflict with the queen, who he so admired, and had a profound effect on his relationship with her. However, it is possible that through his overtly pompous and pretentious display in 1559, Lord Dudley was able to guarantee more political support in England for Elizabeth than that of any foreign match. But for Burghley, almost any suitor for the queen's hand, whether in England or abroad, was preferable to the idea of Dudley sitting on a throne next to her.[16]

The conflict between Burghley and Dudley is interesting, as it not only refers to the courtly language of love and worship of Elizabeth in all her divinity but also indicates a real struggle for power and influence between two men the queen favoured most. It is well known that she invented nicknames for her favourites. As she would later amorously refer to the Duke of Anjou as her 'Frog', she had nicknames for Burghley and Dudley long before she ever considered alliance in matrimony with France. Burghley was 'Sir Spirit', Walsingham, her Secretary of State, was referred to as 'Moor', and Dudley was often called her 'sweet Robin', 'Rob', or her 'eyes'. Here, the contrast between the nicknames can indicate a hierarchy in the queen's affections. For instance, Robert Dudley appearing to have more than one nickname could indicate that their relationship was more than that of two childhood companions, and more than the political. If, at best, the queen and her 'eyes' were lovers in a sense of chaste affections. It is also probable that sexual pleasure between the two could exist in ways other than sex. However, this has only been speculated.

In Feria's account to Philip of Spain, it is not only clear that, in terms of ranking, Burghley would for some time remain second to that of Dudley but also that Elizabeth made no mistake in openly showing her favouritism for Dudley, despite his marriage to Amy Robsart. Feria would go on to become a thorn in the queen's side, as it is most likely the case that rumours regarding her intimacy and sexual affair with Dudley began with his reports back to Spain. It is interesting that, by the time Elizabeth was courting the Duke of Anjou, such rumours had faded or disappeared entirely, like so many of the male favourites of her youth. It would seem in many ways that she was blinded by her affections for Dudley and that she risked her position as a female ruler and any future foreign alliances because of this mistake in overt favouritism. It is events such as this that will often bring another, harsher side of her to the surface. As punishment for his reports back to Philip, Feria was not only eventually sent back to the Spanish court, his wife, who was heavily pregnant at the time, was made to stand for a reported two hours whilst waiting on an audience with the queen.[17]

It is this voice of Elizabeth that is often missing from the narrative, including her many verses and romantic correspondence with Anjou. There was a darker and crueller side to her that many close to her would witness, yet due to the glory and success of her reign, this important trait in the Virgin Queen is often overlooked. However, in order to understand the Elizabeth of her later reign and her seemingly genuine affections for her 'Frog' Anjou, her relationship with Dudley and the effects of its openness on politics and the English court must be taken into account.

Elizabeth was a pragmatist, and for all her affection and pompous flirtations with Dudley, it is unlikely she would have considered entering into a sexual relationship outside the sanctity of marriage. Her own strong religious morality must be considered, along with her existing reputation as an illegitimate princess based on her father's break from Rome, divorce from Katherine of Aragon, eventual marriage to her mother, Anne Boleyn, and the latter's untimely downfall and execution. It must also be noted that during the reign of her sister Mary, Elizabeth was yet again bastardized in the eyes of the Catholic Church and, thus, any dishonour and stain attached to her childhood and early adolescence must have remained in her memory, as well as the collective memory of her courtiers, councillors, and foreign rivals.

This factor allows for an understanding of her attachment to Anjou later in life, when any hope of bearing an heir had probably long gone. It is possible that, by this time, Elizabeth was either attempting to make up for her stubbornness in the past regarding matrimony and childbearing, or she simply longed for some form of romantic relationship later in life. Perhaps Anjou presented a second chance of love? It would become clear by 1560, specifically Sunday 8th September that any hope of a marriage with Dudley after the death of his wife was impossible.

Ironically, though it was only possible for she and Dudley to marry if Amy Robsart were to die, it was precisely the event of her death, or, rather, the suspicious circumstances surrounding it, that would make any match between the queen and her 'eyes' impossible. Amy had been staying at Cumnor Place in Oxfordshire when, on the morning of her death, she had insisted that all her servants vacate the house and attend a fair being held in Abingdon. When her household returned later that afternoon, they found her lifeless body at the bottom of a short flight of spiral stairs, with her neck broken and two small wounds to her head. It would seem that, no matter the success of Elizabeth's reign, nor the adoration of many suitors and her court, the possibility of her finding happiness, in love at least, was to be continuously diminished by one weakness – 'her sweet Robin'.

The coroner's verdict indicated that, though misfortunate, Amy's death was an accident: '...by reason of the accidental injury or of that fall and of Lady Amy's own body weight falling down the aforesaid stairs, the same Lady Amy there and then broke her own neck, on account of which certain fracture of the neck the same Lady Amy there and then died instantly...'[18]

Despite the coroner's verdict, Dudley was immediately

suspected of either murdering his wife himself, or having plotted to have her assassinated. Due to the suspicions of the court and the general public, he took care to uncover the true nature of Amy's death. Yet, despite all his efforts and those of many modern researchers and historians, whether Amy's death was an accident, suicide, or due to a murder plot, it has never quite been resolved. It is unlikely that Elizabeth or Dudley would be in any doubt of the consequences of murdering his wife, and yet the debate continues.

It is believed rumours had already begun in court of Dudley's plot to murder his wife so he could marry the queen without any obstacle. Again, here existed the suspicion that he was simply waiting for his wife to die, as, by 1560, many knew that she was gravely ill.[19] What also fuelled such views was the fact that by the time of Elizabeth's coronation in 1559, the couple were already estranged and had separated. It was well known that he visited his wife but once a year and, astonishingly, when he was permitted to leave court and attend to her in her illness, Elizabeth insisted that he wear all black and was 'to do nothing with her'.[20] What this meant exactly is uncertain. It could be suggested that she meant for no sexual relations to take place between them. Yet, there is no reason to suggest that she should want to deny Dudley his rights as Amy's husband, as the queen could hardly indulge in his advances herself.

Prior to this scandal, Elizabeth was also on her deathbed earlier that year and expected to die when she contracted smallpox. When, at her worst state during this illness, the Virgin Queen declared that, though she did love Dudley deeply, nothing of ill-repute had occurred between them, God as her witness.[21] So, though it seems that the queen herself did not, nor could not, secretly order the death of Amy Robsart, the possibility of Dudley orchestrating his wife's death cannot be dismissed. Many were suspicious of the report that he dined with Robert Smith – once a servant of Elizabeth's and foreman of the jury investigating Amy's death – on the night before the verdict of 'accidental death' came about.

It is almost certain that Elizabeth would have been aware of any attempts on Dudley's part to rid himself of an already ailing wife to secure a marriage for them. Though it is impossible to get to the truth of the matter, it is likely that she took some time to consider the possibility of matrimony between herself and her favourite after the scandal. In the end, as was typically the case with the Tudors, she chose her position and duty as queen over her feelings for Dudley. Though she must have brooded upon the consequences for some time, she decided that she must put ideas of a marriage aside, as well as distance herself from him. For a while, at least. However, it would seem that, though she was madly in love with him, she had decided prior to her ascension that she would never marry.

The queen often left hints for her courtiers and advisors regarding her feelings towards marriage. When the likes of Burghley would push her too far and attempt to pressure her to secure the succession by marrying and providing an heir, she would proclaim that she already had a husband: 'the Kingdom of England'.[22] Camden recorded these very words in his *Annales,* although it is widely believed that he thought them up himself. It is far more likely that Elizabeth actually stated: 'In the end, this shall be for me sufficient, that a marble shall declare that a queen, having reigned such a time, lived and died a virgin'.[23] Yet, though it would now seem a match between the queen and her favourite was impossible, she was not wanting for company. Perhaps the only time she was ever truly alone was in her dreams as she slept at night. Though, whether she slept well at this point, is questionable. She was constantly and contently surrounded by her ladies of the bedchamber and maids of honour, and she openly admitted this.[24] The fact that she remained a virgin and an unmarried queen was not only unheard of during the period, it was entirely unprecedented that a woman would ever have the inclination to rule alone, in her own right. However, due to her apparent fragility in the eyes of her male contemporaries, until she found a suitable husband, it was absolutely obligatory that she should be accompanied by her ladies at all times to avoid any slander on her name and a dint in her reputation. It is important to remember, after all, that any slur upon her reputation could hinder any future prospect of matrimony.[25]

Elizabeth's female attendants were not only essential for her reputation, they were also her personal servants. She had two separate groups of attending ladies – the first serving her in public at court whilst she was attending to her own duties, referred to as 'the ladies in the presence chamber', and the second serving her 'privately' and referred to as 'the maids of honour'. However, the maids of honour had the queen's favour and often attended to her needs or simply accompanied her when she went on royal procession. It is also likely that Elizabeth hand-picked these ladies and was aware that if she was to rule and govern alone, she was better to surround herself with women she could not only trust but count on to keep her company and cheerful during a lonely reign.

Yet, it can be said that they did not always succeed in all of these duties. Few men were ever granted the privilege of entering the queen's bedchamber. But one man, John Astley, or Ashley, the husband of her favourite maid of honour and perhaps best friend and mother figure, Kat, rose to great favour and was present in her private rooms with his wife for much of Elizabeth's early reign. These positions broke down into smaller ones within her privy chamber staff. There were ladies of the bedchamber, gentlewomen of the chamber, and chamberers. All together, these ladies counted to about sixteen or seventeen.[26]

Kat would remain her favourite lady until her death in 1565, and was succeeded by Blanche Parry, who had actually attended Elizabeth when she was an infant, and a mere princess in comparison to the queen she would become. Yet, she had another favourite, and although she selected her companions carefully, and enjoyed giving high positions to family members, she would come to regret giving the position of lady of the bedchamber to her cousin, Lettice Knollys.[27] Lettice was the daughter of Katherine Knollys, nee Carey, and thus, granddaughter of Elizabeth's aunt, Mary Boleyn – her mother's sister – once mistress to Henry VIII. Little is known about the life of Lettice's parents, Katherine and Henry, but it is known that they met in court around 1539, three years after Anne Boleyn's fall from grace. They were married by 1540, and Lettice was their third child. Katherine and Lettice were close, thus her appointment as Elizabeth's lady of the bedchamber seems unsurprising.[28] Yet, Lettice would unleash a betrayal of the queen so monumental and scandalous that she was banished from court and never returned to fill any personal duty thereafter.

Following his wife's scandalous death, Dudley continued to pursue the queen for her hand in marriage, though she had for some time distanced herself from him. Yet, while she never gave in, her feelings for her 'sweet Robin' would never entirely diminish, and, indeed, he had come closer than any other man. That is until she met the Duke of Anjou some time later. For years, she would give Dudley false hopes, until, a decade or so after the death of his wife, he came to the realization that their marriage would never come into being. As time went on, their courtly love would change and develop into something different – a deep friendship. Yet, Elizabeth's possessiveness is evident in the events that were to transpire. It is speculated that Lettice, though already married to Walter Devereux, was often flirtatious with the queen's favourite, and had even angered her once in doing so.

It would seem that, like with the demise of Amy Robsart, the death of Lettice's husband Walter would have a profound influence on the queen's relationship with her two favourites, as they were about to embark on a path that would ultimately betray their mistress and unknowingly shape the course of history. By September 1576, perhaps based on the findings of his physician or the continuation of pains to the stomach and abdomen, Lettice's husband was aware that he would never recover, and began to settle his estate. He even wrote to the queen, stating his hour of judgement was approaching.[29] By 22nd September, Lettice was a widow, and her flirtations with the queen's favourite would soon develop into something much more. It can be suggested that, by early 1577, Dudley intended on marrying her. Some would even suggest that, yet again, he had removed any obstacle well in advance of his intentions for matrimony; it was speculated that he had Walter poisoned.[30] Although, it seems more likely that he would be all too aware that such an undertaking would not only jeopardize any prospect of marriage between himself and Lettice, it would also force him further from Elizabeth's favour, and thus further from power. Therefore, Camden's clever insinuations of Dudley's role in the demise of Walter seem unfounded and borne out of court gossip.

If not by 1577, then by the beginning of 1578, Lettice and Dudley most likely would have entered into a secret contract of marriage. Her interest in Dudley as a new suitor may not only have been due to his reported good looks and charm but also because of his high position in the queen's favour, a high income, and numerous estates. This was certainly an advantageous match for a queen's lady, who was also a daughter of the rumoured bastard of Henry VIII. The attraction for Dudley was also similar: Lettice came from a good Protestant family, she was obviously capable of producing children – evident from her marriage to Walter – and it is important to note that any possibility of Henry VIII's blood running through her veins may have enticed his advantageous nature. However, regardless of what he and Lettice thought in terms of a good match, the queen would never have approved, and they knew it.[31]

Although they knew they were tempting fate, it seems that

their passions went above duty for the queen. A risky business, considering Elizabeth had often sent her own family members to the Tower, even despite pregnancies, for fear of any match spiking a higher claim to the throne than hers. By September 1578, Lettice and Dudley were married, and though it was the surest way of losing the queen's favour, the match would turn out to be a relatively happy one, despite Elizabeth's anger and Lettice's subsequent banishment. Lettice could never go back on her decision, and her relationship with her cousin and queen would change forever.[32]

These events would also have a profound effect on Elizabeth's bond with Dudley, and though she loved him and valued his friendship, their relationship would diminish and take another form. Interestingly, all of this took place during the talks of a French match and alliance through marriage between the queen and Anjou, though any affection for him, whether real or not by this time, could never lessen her admiration and love for Dudley.[33]

By the time Anjou came into the picture, rumour of the betrayal of the queen's 'eyes' and his new wife was not only rife amongst the court but it allowed for the possibility of the French duke triumphing over all of Elizabeth's suitors, including Dudley. Not that the ageing forty-five-year-old queen had many suitors left at this point. It seems that the next events to play out were either due to the planning of Anjou himself or his personal envoy, Monsieur Jean de Simier, who was sent to Elizabeth's court in January of 1579. As Nicola Tallis points out, Simier was the perfect candidate to help Anjou's pursuit to woo the virgin queen.[34] He was not only the Duke's close friend but was also charming and skilled in the courtly dance of love and worship – something once very familiar to Elizabeth, considering her cult of courtly amour that had begun during her early reign. Though Camden can often be taken with a pinch of salt, it is important to note that he, too, mentioned the effects of Simier's visit to Elizabeth: '...a most choice courtier, exquisitely skilled in love toys, pleasant conceits and court dalliances...'[35]

Simier was also the perfect candidate to bring on the fall of Lettice, if not Dudley also. It was his scheming (something evidently second-nature to him) that would reveal the poisonous chalice in the queen's hand. At the same time, both Lettice and her new husband found the idea of a match between their mistress and a French Catholic too much to swallow, made worse by a mutual dislike and distrust for Simier. Whatever the reason, as it has been widely speculated upon, Simier revealed to Elizabeth the details of the courtship and marriage between Dudley and Lettice. He told her that Dudley, who had by this point been well established in his appointment as the Earl of Leicester, was not worthy of her favour, and was wrong to oppose any match between herself and the Duke of Anjou. To add to this, he informed her that it was also the case that the queen's favourites had betrayed her in matrimony, and Lettice, the queen's own kinswoman, was now not only the Countess of Essex but also of Leicester. This horrified Elizabeth, and shook her to her core. By this point, she had not intended to further her past intention to consider marriage between herself and Dudley but, perhaps now, she realized that his attention would no longer be fixated on her and her needs, rather on those of his new wife – her servant.

Camden also revealed that Elizabeth's reaction was so bad that she ordered Dudley to be 'committed to the Tower...'[36] However, luckily for the newlyweds, the Earl of Sussex dissuaded the furious queen in her anger. While the couple were spared the horror of the Tower, they were both ordered to make themselves sharply absent from court, though it would seem Lettice bore the brunt of the queen's wrath. The reasons for this are unclear, although it can be assumed, due to Elizabeth and Lettice's likeness, and shared qualities, the ageing queen was probably more hurt that the only man who ever came close to marrying her in the past twenty years had betrayed her for a younger version of herself.

Rather than showing genuine remorse for her actions and betrayal of her mistress, Lettice stood firm against her. This behaviour was unwise and it landed her in even hotter water. Elizabeth was the queen, Lettice was not, and the monarch would remind her of that. Shortly after the scandal was revealed to the queen, both she and Lettice brought an end to their once-close relationship in a dramatic confrontation. Again, there seems a darker and violent side to Elizabeth that is rarely revealed, shown on this occasion when she reputedly boxed Lettice's ears while screaming 'as but one sun lightened the earth, she would have but one queen in England'. However, regardless of Lettice and Dudley's disgrace, Elizabeth would eventually have to accept their marriage. Though he remained in her affections and would eventually regain favour, Lettice would never be welcomed back to court and was banished to the shadows forever.[37] The relationship between the queen and her 'sweet Robin' would also never be the same as it once was, and it is possible that this factor influenced her courtship with, and intentions to marry, her 'Frog' – the Duke of Anjou.

Chapter 2

The Pursuit of a Queen

For the first two decades of Elizabeth's reign, marriage was a constant topic of discussion, debate, and often dread. By the time any mention of marriage between the queen and Anjou came about, she was most likely in no condition for conceiving, let alone giving birth to a child. Any pretences that she would accept a suitor and secure the succession and the continuation of the Tudor dynasty were slowly dissolving. So, it must have taken her courtiers and advisors by surprise when she seemed to show interest in a match with Anjou. As will become clearer, Elizabeth began this courtship with an agenda. However, you will also see that it would eventually become more than the typical show of love between England and a foreign match in pursuit of a political alliance.

Regardless of whether she ever really intended to marry or not, and forgetting her words in 1559 regarding this, it is important to remember that marriage was an important factor, which her foreign alliances relied on.[1] Though her suitors numbered greatly in her youth compared to that of her later years, the queen and her council often found liabilities in particular foreign suitors. In a way, if it were not for the scandal surrounding the death of Amy Robsart, a match with Dudley may have eventually been negotiated, despite Burghley's opposition due to the earl's overt improvidence in Elizabeth's favour.

The queen's speech regarding her 'marriage to England' led to the formation of her very public identity as the 'Virgin Queen', and though it would have been her intention to create this image of purity – considering the destruction of her parents' marriage – for her own religious and personal reasons, some feel that this was not a vow of celibacy. There are those who believe that Elizabeth's utility of foreign proposals, and the fact that she welcomed them at all, argues against any idea of her vowing celibacy in 1559. However, it is important to note that, as queen, and as a woman, she would have been encouraged by her counsellors and, perhaps, pushed by Burghley, to receive her suitors' letters and portraits along with their ambassadors and envoys. It is notable that she further encouraged negotiations of marriage overseas on many occasions by sending portraits of herself between 1567 and 1581, the latter year indicating her last suitor and, perhaps, only official courtship with Anjou.[2]

At some point in May of 1559, some six months after her ascension and the death of her sister Mary I, her sever from Spain was yet to come about. Interestingly, though now the widower of Mary I, and no longer king-consort and de facto co-ruler of England, Philip was inclined to, or rather persuaded to, propose marriage to the young, charismatic twenty-six-year-old queen, despite their overt religious differences, amongst other factors. It seems that, in terms of an alliance with and influence over England, one queen was just as good as another. Perhaps it was Feria who persuaded him to propose a match in order to keep a strong tie between England and Spain.

Philip's wooing of the new queen, or rather his attempt to woo her, seems to come from a genuine interest in England politically, and so it can be stated that his intentions were solely political and completely absent of genuine affection and romance. Elizabeth's initial reception of his attempt at courtship also shows her consideration to keep English and Spanish relations on good terms, yet it is unlikely that she would have considered ever marrying her sister's widower. Considering her feelings regarding matrimony in 1559, it is not surprising that she failed to go ahead with any marriage, never mind one with the man she once considered her brother-in-law.[3] It cannot be said for sure whether she gave an eventual refusal of a match, or if Philip ultimately decided to withdraw his proposal. It can be suggested that he found the idea of the match unsuitable at one point prior to being persuaded by Feria. When Feria returned home due to the displeasure of Elizabeth, it was almost certain that an alliance, whether that be general or in matrimony, would remain unaccomplished.[4]

It must also be noted that during the reign of Mary I, Philip sought to marry Elizabeth off to a foreign suitor that would benefit both England and Spain by means of political alliance. His first choice, Emmanuel Philibert, the Duke of Savoy, had connections with the Habsburg cause in Italy. He was a staunch Catholic, the right age, and of royal blood. However, this would have imposed a threat not only to Elizabeth's succession, her own personal feelings regarding religion, but also to the Protestant cause in England.[5] As it turned out, neither Mary nor Elizabeth would agree to the match, and, despite their differences and difficult relationship, their shared decision on such matches would have a profound effect on English history that Mary would never have been able to predict, nor Elizabeth have dreamt of, at that time.

Regarding his own match with Elizabeth later on, Philip was worried about the French reaction, suspecting that they would see the marriage as a direct act of provocation. This could not be allowed, as it would entice the continuation of the French war with Spain. Most notably, however, the idea of an alliance through matrimony with a queen he viewed as a heretic, was too much for him to stomach. It was suggested that Elizabeth should convert to Catholicism if a marriage agreement came about.[6] She, however, would certainly not have agreed to this and, therefore, it seems that a match was opposed on both sides. This eliminated any potential alliance between England and Spain, and allowed for a series of events that would challenge the might of Spain as a European power, and establish England and Elizabeth as a mighty nation under the rule of a Protestant, a woman, and a virgin.

Throughout her sister's disastrous reign, it is clear that by being implicated in numerous plots and rebellions, Elizabeth would have been under a great deal of stress. Though it may seem that she had, at the very least, been in contact with the conspirators, it is unlikely that she would have given her consent to such rebellions, on paper anyway. Anna Whitelock points out that Elizabeth often excused herself from Mary's summons.[7] Yet, in terms of incriminating evidence, her lack of a reply and refusal to attend her sister's presence does not implicate her. In fact, far from indicating her role in or sanction of any plot, Elizabeth's attempts to excuse herself from the queen's presence indicates that she feared going to court where she would be either watched or imprisoned. Regardless of her resistance, she was eventually formally charged in the Wyatt conspiracy and sent to the Tower, later to be released on house arrest.

It is unsurprising that she was unwilling to enter a marriage that her sister had orchestrated in the hope of getting her out of the way, and it can also be suggested that, due to the incredible stress she was under during this period of her life, marriage would have been the last thing on her mind. She often spoke of her wish to remain single, and though the popular myth of the virgin queen existed even during her own reign, it could be debated whether these statements reflected her true feelings about love and marriage. It is possible that she expressed her wish to remain single during her sister's reign for political as well as religious reasons. However, as a European princess and Mary's de facto heir, she would have thought it unwise to outwardly reject any suitor for fear of it being taken as an insult.[8] As queen, she would use these same tactics to avoid matrimony but remain in the game in order to keep up appearances that she was marriageable and politically open to alliances. After all, as a queen and Protestant, she needed strong political ties within Europe. This is probably why she and Philip played into the idea of a match, as both possibly wanted to avoid the breakdown of English and Spanish relations. However, we now know their efforts to remain aligned politically, without marriage negotiations, would fail.

Again, during Mary's reign, Philip was eager to promote another of his relations, Eric, the son of then King Gustavus Vasa of Sweden, as a possible match for Elizabeth. Mary I disfavored the idea, as did Elizabeth. However, in November of 1557, the King of Sweden sent an envoy to England to discuss the possibility of a match between his son and Elizabeth, amongst other political proposals. In a direct insult towards Mary, the envoy went straight to Elizabeth with a letter from the prince to seek her approval. This infuriated Mary, who was only reassured when Elizabeth turned the offer down.[9]

However, within the first year of her reign, she was to receive a proposal of marriage again from the now King Eric. This time, it seems that, instead of an outright refusal, she used a tactic of offering 'fair words', which would have kept him interested, without her having to give a final answer for some time. This was a tactic she would later use when negotiations of an alliance in marriage between England and France began, with Anjou as the proposed match. However, it would be this proposal from Anjou that eventually saw her letting her guard down as her affections grew. When Eric wrote to her on 25th February 1560, indicating his intentions to visit her, she panicked. She rushed off a reply, stating that she regrettably did not share his feelings, and that he should not visit England:

A letter truly yours both in the writing and sentiment, was given us on 30 December by your very dear brother, the Duke of Finland. And while we perceive therefrom that the zeal and love of your mind towards us is not diminished, yet in part we are grieved that we cannot gratify your Serene Highness with the same kind of affection. And that indeed does not happen because we doubt in any way of your love and honour, but, as often we have testified both in words and in writing, that we have never yet conceived a feeling of that kind of affection towards any one.[10]

Elizabeth also spoke honestly in this letter of her intentions to remain single, which she enjoyed. She also stated that, for the present time, she did not wish to take a husband, and asked that Eric would not wait on her to change her mind. In many ways, this was Elizabeth at her most honest. Though she stated that she did not hold any affection for him, it is clear that she cared enough to spare the young king the embarrassment or ridicule that would come from attempting to court a queen who had no desire to marry.

While this letter reflects that she had no intentions to marry, it could also be taken to indicate she had no intention to marry an absent husband, as her sister had. It is also clear that she did not want to part with her already existing husband – that being the Kingdom of England.[11] All of these factors could conclude that though she enjoyed the single life, and the courtly cult of love forming around her, she had a mind to refuse courtship when the match did not suit her needs. However, she was also keen to keep negotiations open for political reasons. This does not mean that she was wholly opposed to marriage, as has been often stated, but that she was simply waiting for the right suitor to come about that would allow her to hold onto her own personal power. It is also probable that her affections for Dudley, despite their distance by 1560 due to his wife's suspicious death, had a profound effect on her ability to negotiate marriage elsewhere. Indeed, it seems that Dudley's secret marriage to Lettice Knollys, the queen's own kinswoman, would, in a way, free her in regards to any possible guilt she felt in humouring marriage proposals.

She possibly had other reasons to make a swift rejection of Eric's attempts to court her in person. Tracy Borman makes an excellent point that Elizabeth was also using this letter to her advantage in terms of dulling any rumours in her own court and abroad, that she had any involvement in Amy Robsart's death. However, though this tactic did work for a short time, it backfired when rumours circulated that her refusal of Eric was due to her relationship with and intention to marry Robert Dudley.[12] It can now be assumed that her rejection of Eric would not only allow for her later courtship with Anjou to begin but it is also clear that the match would probably have ended in tears. Eric's tears. Though he was a good match in that he was a young king, handsome, and, most importantly, Protestant, not to mention that the marriage would have secured trade routes beneficial to both nations, a family secret existed that could have been detrimental to Elizabeth's reign. The Vasas family seem to have suffered from some form of mental illness, invoking great paranoia. Perhaps some form of schizophrenia.

Like his father, Eric would later succumb to this inherited madness. By 1567, only several years after his attempts to woo Elizabeth, he had become extremely paranoid in terms of his position and personal safety. He is said to have imagined many plots of rebellion, and, eventually, he personally murdered a number of courtiers who served in high-ranking positions. His brothers would ultimately depose him, having him poisoned to death in 1577.[13] So it would seem Elizabeth unknowingly got herself out of a possible threatening position that could have endangered her safety as well as the national security of her realm.

Eric's attempts to court her have been carried down through history and have left an interesting legacy in literature, as Lisa Hilton has mentioned. The musical manuscripts commonly known as the Winchester Part Books were made up of a number of sonnets that were a production of French chansons set to Italian madrigals. In this, they were uniquely of a Renaissance nature, and romantic. Eric's way of showing Elizabeth that he could play the romantic role of courtly love that her court had adopted may have surprised her. It is known that her courtly cult of love was well spoken of in Europe, and so it seems unsurprising that Eric chose this path of courtship. Interestingly, the legacy of this courtship began by the use of several tunes from the manuscript in Philip Sidney's *Certaine Sonnets* in 1570, which Hilton rightly states were a 'plaintive echo' of Eric's hopeless attempts to woo the defiant virgin queen.[14]

In terms of the best possible match, Archduke Charles of Austria was a strong candidate. In terms of diplomacy, this potential marriage could prove to be useful for Elizabeth. By around 1566, she was under enormous pressure to take a husband. Far from lacking any real interest in marriage or child-bearing during the first couple of years of her reign, it seems that the queen began to seriously consider the future of her realm and the importance of a successor. It would also seem that, besides that of her advisors and the members of the commons, her people, in general, were hopeful that she would eventually marry in order to bring about an heir. As her lords and members of the commons began to discuss negotiations of a match with Charles of Austria, it must have looked inevitable at times that she would eventually have to succumb to her fate as a ruling woman and produce an heir. It is possible that a part of her even wanted to.

Regardless of the pressure put on her from her closest advisors and government, she would have been deeply troubled if they had suggested she did not care about the future of the realm, and therefore she must have, at times, looked back on the reigns of her father and grandfather and considered that taking a husband and producing an heir were not only her duty but best for the future of the dynasty her father worked so hard to preserve.[15]

She found the match with Archduke Charles too much to take on, considering that he was of Hapsburg lineage. Her government and advisors were becoming exasperated in their attempts to fully convince her to marry, and to find her a suitable match she would deem agreeable. As the queen aged, time was running out. During the period of negotiations with Austria, her advisors pushed her too far and she spoke openly of her feelings towards marriage:

> I will never break the word of a prince spoken in public place, for my honour sake. And therefore I say again, I will marry as soon as I can conveniently, if god take not him away with whom I mind to marry, or myself, or else some other great let happen...And I hope to have children, otherwise I would never marry.[16]

It is also evident that while Elizabeth may have been willing to marry, she was not willing to agree to a match with a Catholic, for the Catholic religion represented not only the bloody burnings of her late sister's reign but also a step backwards from the preservation and continuation of the Protestant faith, which gave England so much independence politically.[17] This is probably why the queen would later ponder on the consequences of a possible match with Anjou, who she not only admired but felt a profound connection to, despite their many differences.

The expectation that she should marry was an enormous pressure to bear, yet she did so alone, for her entire reign. Regardless of her many suitors, for a time she was a shining example of what a woman could be when given a position of power. However, the constant pressure to accept her fate as a queen and woman had to have a detrimental effect, along with the idea that, as a wife, she would no longer rule England alone. Nor could she rule her husband, and, again, if she married, she could lose her own personal power. Burghley continued to advise her that marriage was in the best interest of the realm, and though he often felt his words had some effect, he would soon be left disappointed again. He wrote openly in 1564 to a confidant regarding his despair in her refusal to take a husband, stating how he felt the future of the realm hung in the balance, which gave him great discomfort to the point in which he could no longer enjoy life. Later on, when Elizabeth's courtship with Anjou was in motion, though worried at the prospect of a man such as the duke as a potential husband for his queen, he was able to put his own sentiments aside for the sake of the realm, as he felt marriage was the absolute solution.[18]

The idea of a Catholic match for Elizabeth made many of her subjects uneasy. Though she first claimed that she intended to remain 'religiously tolerant', the Elizabethan administration, which was in the hands of Burghley and Walsingham, amongst others, ensured that the remaining Catholic communities were diminished to a number so low, they were often subject to open attack. Religion had influence over Elizabeth's reign in many ways outside of marriage negotiations. The attacks on Catholics had worsened by 1569, when Northern rebels had answered the pope's call after he excommunicated England's 'heretical usurper'. However, many Catholics remained loyal to their monarch, despite their strong faith. Leanda De Lisle notes that many counties, such as Hampshire, remained devoted to the Protestant queen, despite being so stanchly Catholic. So, it seems that, though religion played a part in Elizabeth's decisions to refuse many a suitor, it must be noted that she knew many of her loyal subjects were Catholic.[19] It is important to consider that she also refused offers of marriage from loyal Protestant and noble Englishmen.

However great the hopes of her many Catholic subjects that she would eventually marry Anjou, they would ultimately be disappointed due to strong Protestant opposition. While her personal feelings for Anjou may have mattered, her duty to her realm and the Protestant faith would always come first. Changes to the royal household also indicate that, though religiously tolerant at first, she was anxious to distance herself and her own courtiers from the Catholic faith and Rome itself, where she was deemed an illegitimate daughter of a whore, a heretic, and a usurper of the English Crown. Devout Catholics, such as Lord Hastings and Sir Edward Waldegrave, were removed from their positions upon her ascension, and though this may not seem like the religious tolerance she spoke of, it was probably in the best interests of their safety that many Catholic nobles left court for their country residences or mainland Europe.[20] It seems that much of Elizabeth's household from Hatfield, where she remained under house arrest during the last days of her sister's reign, would remain loyal and follow her to court.[21] With the wars of religion taking hold in Europe, and the massacre of Elizabeth's fellow Protestants in Paris, it is not surprising that, by the time she came into contact with Anjou, there were many divisions amongst the English people on the idea that a match between a Protestant queen and a Catholic duke could solve anything.[22]

By the time negotiations with Anjou began, which would also be her last official courtship, her face had clearly aged – her jawline was squarer, almost gaunt, and the tip of her nose had developed something of a hook. Though she was no longer the youthful queen she had once been, what she lacked in beauty, she made up for in intelligence, decorum, and splendid attire. However, Catherine de Medici dismissed her age and appearance as unimportant, though it must be remembered that she was searching for a suitable bride for her son, which would allow him to rule over Elizabeth and, therefore, England.

Elizabeth was also in need of security. It would appear that Catherine, like the English queen, was a strong woman for her time, and could easily overlook the objections of Burghley. She felt that if Elizabeth was happy to wed her son, despite their age difference, then she could find no fault in the proposal, regardless of religion. Initially, the match was questionable and, apparently, Elizabeth gestured that though she was grateful for the offer, she felt unworthy, and if she were but ten years younger, she would have happily accepted.[23] This seems likely to have been one of her tactics, which would spare her the ordeal of having to marry and also avoid conflict regarding the growing anti-Protestant sentiment raging across Europe. It also meant that by politely declining a match, she was able to keep Catherine as an ally for some time, rather than an opponent.

Anjou was a possible candidate for her hand as early as 1571. However, as she always insisted on seeing a suitor in person prior to making any decision to marry, these first attempts led to nothing, and it was unlikely that she would have taken on Anjou as a husband at this time, anyway, due to his tender age of seventeen. Again, in 1574, Catherine mentioned a possible match but this would also come to nothing. It seems that the negotiations of marriage were not taken seriously until 1579, when Elizabeth would have more reasons to consider such a match other than that of a prince's appearance and manner.[24]

Around this time, as the final negotiations of marriage were taking place, Dudley was in the midst of his own secret marriage with Lettice Knollys. It is ironic that he protested against any match with Anjou, who was then Duke of Alençon, considering he had failed to mention marrying Lettice, Elizabeth's kinswoman.

The queen had reasons for avoiding marriage other than her fears of being ruled by a man, or her feelings for her 'sweet Robin'. In order to gain an insight into her psychological attitude towards marriage, and all that it involved – sexual intimacy, childbearing, and being subdued to the will of her husband – we have to look back on her life as a child and her teenage years. Her serious doubts about the advantages of a marriage, whether English or foreign, are not surprising considering her mother's execution at the hands of her father, Henry VIII, as John Guy notes. And the accusations against Anne Boleyn of adultery and incest with her own brother must have continued to circulate around the court in the form of rumour and scandal as Elizabeth grew up.[25] It is quite likely, too, that, as she was the only surviving child of her parents' marriage, her mother's memory and execution would have still existed in the minds of some of her servants, and it is probable that, as she grew up, she would have been informed about her parents' marriage, how it came about, and how it was destroyed. The fact that she grew up witnessing her father's multiple marriages, which were mostly failures, and the execution of her stepmother, Catherine Howard, it is also possible that the young princess developed an anxiety disorder, triggered by the idea of, and later discussions of, matrimony.

There was, however, a series of much-darker events in Elizabeth's youth that would have deeply affected her psychologically. Within a few weeks of the death of her father, her stepmother Katherine Parr married her true love, Thomas Seymour. Seymour was the uncle of Elizabeth's late half-brother, King Edward VI, who had died in 1553, not yet an adult. He was also, therefore, the brother of Jane Seymour, Henry VIII's third wife and rival of Anne Boleyn. Yet, despite all of these factors, Elizabeth went to live with Katherine and her new husband, and initially settled in well. Seymour was said to have been handsome, seductive, with a strong body and a 'manly shape', all the necessities of the sixteenth-century ideal man.[26] Just as the young princess would have begun to feel comfortable and safe in the home of her stepmother and charming stepfather, it was soon ruined by Seymour calling to her bedchamber early in the morning before she had risen from bed. These visits must have startled Elizabeth from the beginning, and she began to rise earlier than usual so she could be dressed prior to his arrival.[27]

However, his actions would only become worse, and dangerous. If Elizabeth were dressed before he entered her chamber, he would greet her and then strike her on the back or on her buttocks with disturbing familiarity. If she happened to be in her bed, possibly hoping that it would keep him at a distance from her physically, it did nothing to deter him. He went as far one morning as to kiss her while she was still in her bed. It seems that, if the accounts of Elizabeth's favourite maid of honour Kat Ashley are to be believed, these events had been taking place at the beginning of the marriage between Katherine and Seymour, suggesting they had started at Chelsea Manor, perhaps days after their marriage had taken place. This would have had a profound effect on the dowager queen Katherine, who swiftly became pregnant with Seymour's child.[28]

Within a year of Kat being questioned about Seymour's reported 'romps' with Elizabeth, the relationship between Katherine and Elizabeth was not only compromised but the reputations of all three were severely damaged. If there were only a couple of instances of these intrusions on the princess, it is likely that they would never have been known of or discussed outside of the household. However, if they were cause enough for Kat's concern, then Elizabeth herself must have been deeply worried about her safety and reputation. It also seems that, for whatever reason, Katherine for a time played along with Seymour's predatory actions. John Guy mentions a well-known incident that took place in a garden of Katherine and Seymour's household. Seymour is reported to have 'frolicked with Elizabeth' and cut her black gown into 'one-hundred pieces'. This event would prove too scandalous and Elizabeth's reputation was left hanging by a thread.[29]

In these moments, while she should have been enjoying newfound happiness in a loving home, she was propelled into Seymour's perverse world against her wishes, and was morbidly embarrassed by rumours that she was pregnant with his child. Katherine eventually voiced her concerns to her husband but to no avail. It has often been suggested that these flirtations with Elizabeth were due to Seymour's true agenda: to marry her himself.[30] However, as his wife was pregnant and their marriage a relatively happy one, the common tendency to overlook his actions and excuse them as advantageous seems dated and somewhat misogynistic. It must be considered that this predatory-like characteristic of Seymour's was simply a part of who he was as a person.

It is not surprising, considering these troubling events in Elizabeth's youth, that she attempted to control the sexual behaviour of her members at court. Any stain on her servants and courtiers would have been a stain on her own reputation. It is clear that, however hard she tried to control her court, a number of sexual liaisons, affairs, and secret marriages, other than that of Dudley and Lettice Knollys, occurred, sending her into fits of panic and rage. Her parents' marriage, and events of her childhood and teenage years, all seem to have had a profound psychological effect on her attitude towards marriage, sex, intimacy, and courtship. Although she encouraged the language of love amongst courtiers in terms of honouring her as their queen, even a goddess, the courtly cult of love that developed around the virgin queen would witness a number of affairs and marriages she did not approve of.

Mary Shelton, a chambermaid, is an example of one of Elizabeth's ladies 'behaving badly'. She married a widower, John Scudamore, in secret, sometime between 1573 and 1574, which made Elizabeth erupt into a rage. She is reported to have struck Lady Shelton, attacking her with a candle stick and breaking her finger.[31] However, it must be stated that the whole purpose of a large number of ladies serving the queen at court was to educate them and prepare them for their potential future marriages. Elizabeth would have known this. The scandal of secret marriages and lusty affairs, however, proved too much for her to ignore, considering her own mother's persecution and fall from favour based on unproven charges. Along with this, the scandals of her youth would have put her in a position where she had to attempt to keep a moral standard within her court, and especially that of her ladies. Many modern historians and authors have suggested that she was notoriously jealous of any sexual affair that went on between her ladies or even between her favourite, Dudley. But this claim seems flimsy, without any solid foundation. Elizabeth, more than anyone, knew the importance of a lady finding a suitable match, regardless of her own anxieties about marriage. If she failed to marry, that did not mean her ladies should follow suit. On the contrary, most of her ladies returned to court after getting married, anyway, and Mary Shelton was also eventually permitted back and found a position once more.[32]

It seems that marriages only stirred anxiety in the queen when they were conducted without her permission. This was not uncommon with the Tudors. Her father often reprimanded couples who had married without his permission, or individuals who married below or even above their station. It is clear that Elizabeth saw no issue with marriage in general if the proceedings towards it were genuine, open, and of a good moral standing and intention. It could be suggested that she felt the same in terms of her own possible marriage negotiations. This is probably why she favoured Robert Dudley for some time; she knew him, and he knew her. For all it was worth, their feelings for one another were obviously genuine. Though, because it cannot be proven that they had any sexual relationship, their passions were kept under the belt, and their urges repressed. This was until the death of Amy Robsart and the betrayal of her trust, and possibly why she succumbed to the wooing of Anjou in person, years after marriage negotiations had already been approached and rejected.

Regardless of any affection she may have had in her later negotiations of marriage with Anjou, it is clear that, in the beginning, this attempt to court her would possibly occur with the same dalliance as the others. It is somewhat surprising that, though Elizabeth would reject all candidates for marriage throughout her reign, the proposals kept coming. It would seem that the Virgin Queen's qualities were too much to resist. Despite her rough royal upbringing and scandal-packed adolescence, her reputation emerged unscathed in the eyes of European princes. Susan Doran points out that Elizabeth used the many marriage negotiations going on around her to get out of committing to any suitor in particular. The queen's advisors may have been impatient with her but when she rejected suitor after suitor, they were not too worried as there always seemed to be another potential marriage alliance on the horizon.[33]

In terms of the negotiations of marriage as a means of securing the succession, Natalie Mears rightly mentions that the language of courtship during Elizabeth's reign can indicate the true nature of the political side to her marriage negotiations. While her endless refusals and shrewd tactics to avoid a match caused great anxiety for her councillors, the relationship that existed between the queen and her advisors was possibly more nuanced than has been claimed.[34] It has been suggested that she changed the conventional concept of diplomatic negotiations by using the typical characteristics of a 'mistress' as a political weapon to suit her own personal needs as well as the security of England. It has even been stated that this kind of shrewd negotiation fed her ever-growing vanity.

However, Doran, amongst others, has disagreed. It should seem obvious that Elizabeth used the negotiations of marriage to serve her political interests. But the idea that she conducted herself in a fashion that resembled that of a mistress dangling her goods for all her suitors to grapple over, seems a step too far.[35] This is because such a statement indicates that she saw no other way to negotiate with her allies without the pursuit of marriage being a primary objective. This theory also fails to consider her psychology regarding marriage and courtship.

It has also been suggested that, in relation to the match between her and Anjou, she was willing to genuinely negotiate marriage without pretence because, by this time, England was in need of a strong ally and protector. This seems valid, and it is quite clear that she ruled with her head rather than her heart, as

Doran has suggested.

Few argue that Elizabeth felt any real affection for Anjou. Though it would seem that, initially, she did use this match as a means of relaxing the anxieties of her council and to form an alliance with France that could protect England, her affections for Anjou would grow deeper than that of a strong political ally. The extent of the affection between them has been widely speculated upon, yet continues to be open for debate. Doran argues that her intentions to marry Anjou were genuine.[36] Though lacking in consideration for the queen's personal feelings, outlined in her own hand, this seems correct. The traditional historiographical representation of her as a frigid, stony, goddess-like symbol of female power needs to be broken down and re-assembled. Elizabeth was not made from stone – she had feelings, a beating heart, with needs and urges like any other woman. Yet, she was not 'any other woman'.

Chapter 3

From Alençon to Anjou

In 1578, marriage negotiations with France resumed, and Elizabeth was yet again presented with a series of marital conditions, which the match depended on. This is what many have referred to as the queen's last chance at finding a suitable match, which would ensure the continuation of the Tudor dynasty and, of course, provide her with a husband and someone to share the remaining years of her life with. Little did they know just how long the queen would go on to reign. Initially, it seems likely that she allowed negotiations of a match with Anjou to come about again due to the bloody wars of religion going on throughout Europe. France, at that time, seemed like a sensible ally. There have been many reasons suggested as to why, at the age of forty-five, she would consider re-entering negotiations. Yet, it would seem this was Elizabeth using her typical marriage tactics to gain influence and ensure the safety of her realm during these violent times. She knew that an alliance with France would draw them away from any *entente* with the Spanish, which would put England's safety as a Protestant country in jeopardy.[1]

Her influence over France was essential, and though she may not have intended to actually marry Anjou at this time, it was most likely assumed by many that the queen was at an age, and in a political position, that would perhaps force her hand in this instance, for the sake of her realm. The French soon sent on their provisions for the match, which Elizabeth would ultimately dislike and dismiss. Simier, the duke's representative at the queen's court, presented her with these conditions. Firstly, the duke's religion had to be dealt with. He was to be allowed to practice Catholicism openly. This was a tricky condition. While she had promised religious tolerance at the beginning of her reign, and could possibly come to terms herself with the duke's religion, to allow him to openly practice his faith in Protestant England, whilst her Protestant brothers and sisters on mainland Europe were being massacred, would cause a scandal. As always, her councillors would never allow this, and as they believed they had the duty to decide whom the queen should marry, she would have known that such an allowance could be dangerous to the stability of the Protestant faith in England.[2]

Another condition was that the duke should be crowned king of England, and granted equal power to that of Elizabeth. This, for the queen, her council, and her people, was an unthinkable notion, which most likely brought a great shudder to Burghley. She wrote to the French Ambassador, Sir Amyas Paulet, that she found these conditions to be to her displeasure and stated 'to insist very peremptorily upon certain articles that have always heretofore been denied such princes as in former time have sought us in way of marriage'.[3]

It has been suggested that she was not only insulted due to the fact that her subjects would not allow him to openly practice Catholicism and rule over them as king, but felt somewhat less important than that of the political importance of the match. This, it has been said, is another example where Elizabeth let her vanity overtake her senses.[4] However, this seems unlikely. Surely, at this stage, despite any letters of amour that may have been coming and going, the queen would have put the security of her own country ahead of her feelings. It is evident from her many years living as a single monarch that she felt it necessary to rule alone until a suitable match came along. This is where the common modern representation of Elizabeth as the virginal demi-goddess can twist the truth regarding her views about marriage later on in her reign.

The Duke of Alençon, later Anjou, was the last son born to Henry II of France and Catherine de Medici on 18th March 1555. This was only three years before Elizabeth's ascension to the throne in 1558, meaning that the duke was a mere infant in comparison to the then twenty-five-year-old queen. Though an alliance between three of their sons and Elizabeth was discussed throughout her reign, it was Anjou who would be the only one to court her, and in person, coming closest to actually marrying the virgin queen. By 1559, when the duke was still a mere boy, the war between France and Spain had already been ongoing for some time. This dispute, and the very real threat from Spain, would never really be resolved during his lifetime.[5]

Anjou would go from a relatively obscure and unimportant figure in the Valois family, to the heir presumptive of the French crown after the death of his father and two of his brothers. His career and importance in terms of foreign policy have been widely discussed by Mack P. Holt, amongst others. Yet, his courtship with Elizabeth has yet to be given the recognition it deserves in terms of his role in determining the potential future of the Tudor dynasty, Anglo-French relations and, most relatively, Elizabeth's happiness. It has often been concluded that, though she wrote beautifully of her affections for him and of her sadness due to the eventual end of the courtship, her fondness for him went no deeper than that of the political.

While it is true that the queen found necessity in this match, that is not to say she felt no affection for him. Though he was no king, Anjou had great power by the time Anglo-French negotiations with Elizabeth had begun its second wave. Reported to be ugly, it is important to note that during the sixteenth century, a man's good features were also determined by his masculinity. If the French minister's reports of the duke are to be believed, his influence and position in one of the richest and powerful royal families in Europe were enough to attract the ageing queen. Anjou was ironically regarded as 'the most powerful prince in Christendom without a crown'.[6]

While he seemed powerful by the time he began courting Elizabeth, it has often been stated that he was a rather unfortunate man, and, as a child and during his adolescence, there were many reports that his features were the object of people's jokes within the French court. It is interesting to note that the duke wasn't born with his later-given Christian name of François, being named 'Hercule' at birth. It was after his father died and when civil war broke out, forcing the new king, Charles IX, and the royal family to travel, that the duke's name would eventually be changed. War seems to have had some power over the many directions the duke's life would take, including leading him to Elizabeth.

Somewhere around the time of his brother's early reign, the duke became ill and was sent back towards Paris, away from the royal family, who were travelling on campaign. Little is known about this illness but a letter survives that was written by the nine-year-old duke, indicating that he was slowly recovering.[7] Upon Catherine's return to Paris, she had her son confirmed as a member of the Catholic Church and he was henceforth known as François, Duke of Alençon.

Some historians have suggested that the young prince suffered from a bout of smallpox, which would explain his appearance later in life and the mockery that accompanied it. Author Peter Ackroyd has stated that Anjou was also mocked at court due to a 'deformity of the spine which belied his nickname of Hercules'.[8] However, though it has been reported that he may have had some form of spinal deformity, it is certainly not the case that 'Hercules' or, to put it correctly, Hercule, was a nickname. Though Ackroyd makes some evidently well-researched remarks on Anjou's appearance and apparent deformity, it must be noted that there is no indication or reference for the origin of this information.

Smallpox would have left deep scars if not treated with care, and it is well known that Elizabeth survived this disease, too, and would bear its memory on her face for the rest of her life. This is why she later resorted to wearing a mask of lead make-up, which grew thicker and thicker as she aged. By the time she met Anjou face to face, her make-up would have been significantly dense. In a way, it could be suggested that, in Anjou, she saw something of herself, considering they had both survived the disease, and each had the scars to prove it. For this reason, she may have felt more comfortable around him; however, we cannot know for certain.

It is interesting that, over the course of time, her views towards marriage would alter depending on the political context or simply her mood. Even so, France would always be on her mind as an ally. She would also continue to be an interest to France or, rather, Catherine de Medici. By 1571, Anjou was around fifteen years old. Though an eligible age for a prince of Valois blood, Elizabeth's age would have been considered an issue by many besides his mother. While these attempts to lure her into France's marital bed failed, they would prove a useful foundation later on when negotiations began for a second time. By 1579/80, Anjou would not only be a most acceptable match, considering he was heir apparent to the Valois throne, he was also older, more mature, and, most importantly, a man. He also showed that he was capable of courting the English Queen. Her feelings about marriage at the beginning of negotiations, when Anjou was a mere boy, cannot be known for sure. It seems that she may have been considering marriage as a useful political tool, as well as a tactic to keep her councilors' groaning at bay. Though it would seem she became truly interested in the second phase, it is hard to tell when exactly she began to feel something more for him. As Carole Levin has pointed out, what Elizabeth said, '…however sincere it may have sounded, was not necessarily what she meant'.[9]

To attempt to understand what her feelings were towards Anjou, and to gain a more nuanced interpretation of their courtship, there must be further context given to the life and experiences of him prior to his arrival in England. During the

Wars of Religion, the duke's own household would rise and decline in fortune. This is an important factor when considering his intentions to wed Elizabeth in the first place. One more factor to consider in relation to his own household and fortune is whether he was a good master, or, to be blunt, whether he was fair and paid his staff's wages. The first official survey of Anjou's household that might be seen as legitimate, and to have followed some systematic format, was conducted in 1572, when the duke was seventeen. By this time, negotiations with Elizabeth had begun in their first official course, with letters between Catherine de Medici and the relatively young queen. His household was made up of 262 persons at this stage, 415 by 1575, and, only one year later, 942.[10] But how much of this growth in fortune and status can really be attributed to the duke himself, rather than his brother and mother?

There is no doubt that when he became Duke of Anjou, Touraine, and Berry, following the edict of pacification, his fortunes were bound to rise. By 1578, his household expanded even greater to 1123 persons. This seems to be the largest number ever recorded in his employ.[11] Though it is well known amongst historians that, towards the end of his life, his fortune would amount equally to that of his failings in positioning himself in an advantageous royal marriage such as that with Elizabeth, it must be remembered that it was his initial great fortune, large household, and vast expanding popularity that would have attracted Elizabeth to reopen marriage negotiations, other than the necessity of securing her succession issues. It is apparent that his growth in household, great fortune, and his title alterations from Duke of Alençon to Anjou coincided with Elizabeth's views that a negotiation in marriage with France was once again necessary. This could again indicate her shrewd nature, considering the political and religious climate. It was no coincidence.

This does not mean that she should be criticised for her tactics. Anjou may have been reportedly ugly and pock-ridden but, by this time, she wasn't the beauty she had once been. So, it would only seem obvious that an Anglo-French match should be considered. By 1580, Anjou was the heir apparent to the French throne, of Valois blood, rich, powerful and, as it would later be confirmed in their correspondence, charming. In many ways, the duke was already a king himself. Pasquier even remarked that Anjou's entourage was so large at one point, that he was *de facto* 'a second king with his own court'.[12] In terms of what the duke was spending by the time of the first negotiations of marriage with Elizabeth, Holt gives an excellent view of his expenditure on wages and pensions in his study of the Anjou household between 1572 and 1578. By the time the second wave of marriage negotiations commenced, Anjou had grown so wealthy that, within six years, his outgoings on wages and pensions alone had risen by 450 per cent.[13]

By the early 1570s, France, too, had its reasons to form an alliance through marriage with England. It is important to note that, at this time, the Duke of Anjou was not the same man of the later negotiations but the man who would become Henry III of France. This is because Charles IX died in 1574, and the succession of Henry III was swift. Alençon became the Duke of Anjou after he ran into some difficulties with the new king, his brother. In 1575, he fled from the French court due to these differences. Catherine and Henry's fears that he might join the Protestant rebellion would come to fruition. Henry was eventually forced to sign a peace settlement, which rewarded Alençon the Duchy of Anjou.[14] The many changes in the French succession and subsequent changes in titles is a factor that has not only confused some historians but also readers and, so, is necessary to point out. It seems likely that France was in far greater need of the match in terms of support for healing religious divisions that not only caused great destruction through war and massacre but also drained the Valois coffers.

Anjou's brother, Charles IX, wanted to heal the wound caused by religious differences, especially considering the legacy of the Massacre of Saint Bartholomew's Day in Paris, 1572. An Anglo-French alliance with England could prove useful in attempts to defeat Spain, which, in terms of religious war, would ultimately all be down to Elizabeth's courage, leadership, tactics, and luck later on in her reign. For now, however, she wished to avoid war with Spain at all costs. Though a Protestant, she never wished to become a glorified champion of the Protestant cause in Europe. As much as she enjoyed the attentions of her courtiers and suitors, she was ill-at-ease with the idea of intervening in religious conflict because of the great expense, both financially and in human life.[15]

Catherine, the Queen Mother, most likely pushed Charles to discuss negotiations of marriage with England. For whatever reason, she would continue to seek out such an alliance with Elizabeth for many years. Further study into the political relationship between both women could allow for a deeper insight into the political nature of navigating female power during the sixteenth century. Charles' plan was that Elizabeth would marry Anjou, creating a link not only between France and England but with all the other nations or principalities governed by a royal family connected to the Valois dynasty through marriage. It seemed like the perfect solution to out-manoeuvring mighty Spain and ending the Wars of Religion. There was, however, one catch: the current Duke of Anjou, Henry, was decades younger than Elizabeth. Thus, it is understandable that he did not want to marry England's virgin queen, then approaching her forties.

This response would have been rather embarrassing for Elizabeth but a solution existed. François, then Duke of Alençon, who is referred to as simply Anjou in this work, was a few years younger than his brother, and less of an obstinate youth. As mentioned before, Elizabeth initially began to doubt any alliance in marriage with France. However, a treaty was signed on 19th April 1572, that would have made this alliance legitimate, if it were not for the events that would take place in the Netherlands. The negotiations between Catholics and Protestants were getting nowhere. Elizabeth was fearful of committing fully to the match, considering the political circumstances and the chaos in the Royal Council in Paris over religion. She was careful not to provoke Philip of Spain.

Hilton agrees with the general conclusion that the queen used the Anglo-French alliance to keep Philip at bay and, thus, the Spanish at a distance from England. It is also evident from the failures of the Blois-Treaty that she continued to dangle both foreign counterparts, ensuring a marriage chase between Spain and France. Though her marriage negotiations with Spain were by this time over, it was a clever enough tactic, allowing her to hold out as long as possible. Keeping the French and Spanish guessing over the match with Anjou would also have kept Philip out of the Netherlands, and this was a political advantage for Elizabeth and Anjou. The Dutch recruiting Anjou to rule over the Netherlands in Principality changed everything for her. If she married Anjou, she could have had some real influence, and England would be safe from Spain.[16] However, though he seemed a good candidate because of his wealth and power in the Netherlands, and she found this attractive, it was inevitable that his newfound position and career was precariously costly.

Though his wealth had grown substantially, considering his eventual rise in the succession of France, his position as Prince of the Netherlands during a time of war and political-religious strife proved extremely expensive. Luckily, during his courtship with Elizabeth, this was not an issue due to the vastness of his wealth but, by the time of his death, his debts grew to an amount so great it would take several years for his arrears to be paid off. It is also noted by Holt that during this period of his courtship with Elizabeth and his rise to that of a prince in his own right – a *de facto* king in all but name – his military campaigns, grand number of household officers, servants, and expanding court, all added to the slowly declining wealth within his coffers. His trip to England to pursue his courtship with Elizabeth in 1579 would have also had a negative effect on his personal finances.[17]

The Massacre of Saint Bartholomew's Day may have paused the initial marriage negotiations, which may have been for the best. At this point, the duke wasn't yet involved in the French and Spanish interests in the Netherlands and, thus, would have proven a weak companion for Elizabeth. When the prospect of marriage came up again when he was the Duke of Anjou, Simier was dispatched to England, and this would have been to the queen's liking. It seems that Simier lavished her with gifts as well as the duke's letters. She is said to have given Simier a nickname, as she usually did with those she favoured, referring to him as 'Singe' or 'Monkey', which probably did not go down well with him.[18] However, her favour for him would have been noted by the French, and by Anjou himself. This is likely to have fueled his attempts to woo the ageing queen, who, for some time, had been without a suitor and had relied for a number of years on her favouritism for Dudley, Earl of Leicester, though her passion for him in a romantic regard had probably cooled.

She may have had fair intentions in terms of her match with Anjou when negotiations began again in 1579 but she also may not have. Though it would seem that, by the end of their courtship, she did have feelings for him, perhaps out of real love, perhaps out of an ageing woman's desperation to end her life in matrimony – we cannot be sure. It is clear, however, that once letters began to fly between them, and with the aid of Simier's charm, the queen was soon growing more and more committed to the prospects of marriage. But if negotiations had not worked when the duke was younger, and the queen considerably more capable of bearing children, was there a point to this match other than the national safety of England, with France gaining the upper hand somewhat? In terms of physical aesthetic, was Elizabeth attracted to Anjou?

Certainly, she found him charming prior to their meeting. His letters would have pleased her vanity and, with Simier whispering sweet nothings into her ear about Anjou's charm and power, it is not surprising that, by the time they came face to face, she was already somewhat attracted to his character, if not his appearance. But what did he actually look like? If Ackroyd's interpretation of him is to be believed, along with most modern interpretations. the duke was not at all pleasing to the eye. Many would have thought him entirely unsuitable for the match, not only because he was French and because of his age but because of his pock-ridden face. In comparison to the Earl of Leicester, he may have been considered hideous.

The portrait of the duke from 19th March 1572, may be a younger representation of him at the beginnings of the first negotiations to wed him to Elizabeth after his brother's refusal. It is known to be a definite depiction of him, as it is inscribed with the date, his name and age, and states that he was the son of Henry II, King of France. It isn't known for sure who painted this portrait, so it is difficult to obtain any inclination of its likeness to his actual appearance. The painting was first attributed to the artist François Clouet, and then to Frans Pourbus the Elder, but by the early 1950s, scholars came to the conclusion that the artist should remain anonymous, though it was accepted that it was most likely painted by an artist under the influence of the School of Fontainebleau.[19] While it is difficult to say whether Anjou really looked like this in 1572, it is important to mention, as it is one of the few likenesses of him in existence. It is possible that a miniature of the duke based on this portrait was sent to her during the first marriage negotiations. She liked to know what her suitor looked like, and though she would not see him until many years later, this portrait could have resembled the duke in his youth, though, most definitely, the artist thought twice about keeping any possible disfigurement of the face or back in a commission as grand as this.

As the Wars of Religion intensified, so did negotiations of marriage. Between March and April, Elizabeth had been playing her usual tactics with her courtly cult of love that had existed long before the duke was considered a prospective candidate. Though, at this time, she was beginning to warm to the idea of a match with Anjou, helped along by his own hand and Simier's charm, it was still a political matter that would have a role to play in the safety of the realm and the possible succession of the Tudor Dynasty. Despite Anjou's demands to be recognized as king, and to be permitted to openly practice Catholicism, which only created opposition amongst her council and courtiers, Elizabeth eventually gave him safe passage and passport to travel to England to pursue further negotiations in person. Even so, this was done in secret. It would seem that she was eager, excited even, to be courted at her age, especially by a man with power and some influence in the current religious wars. This may have excited her, possibly stretching to mutual affection and respect, because she was probably aware that this was her last chance at marriage. It is also important to note that she must have been aware that if she was ever going to have a child, this was the time, and she had to act fast.

It is also possible that the contents of the duke's letters had some influence over her desires to meet him in person. It has always been stated that Elizabeth ruled with her head rather than her heart. Though it is true that on many occasions she was able to overcome her emotions to do her duty and what was ultimately best for her country, it must be remembered that she was human and, notably, incredibly indecisive. The Spanish Ambassador in London sent word to Philip of Spain in a letter from 24th June 1579, that Elizabeth had granted passage to Anjou. It was noted that the duke's envoy, Monsieur de Rochetaillé, had brought the letter directly to Anjou in France. Though the queen was as ever indecisive, a decision had to be made and, so, the council granted the document of Anjou's passport on 6th July, which would allow his entry into England. Mary Queen of Scots was told that Elizabeth had waited three whole days, with 'many tears', before subscribing Anjou's passport. This may have been due to Dudley's reaction to her serious consideration of the match, where, in anger, he took to his house five miles away, pretending to be ill.[20]

It seems that not everyone at court was convinced of Elizabeth's commitment to the match with Anjou. Even today, speculation exists that she was using the negotiations of marriage with the duke as a ploy to buy more time and to keep in with France. However, this is not the case if the contents of her letters to him beginning from early July have anything to say. The fact that she went against the expressed advice of her council and Dudley's anger to invite Anjou to visit her face to face, can also be attributed to her commitment to the possibilities of marriage at this point, and, most importantly, to the duke.

Chapter 4

The Language of Love

The marriage negotiations between Elizabeth and the Duke of Anjou allow for a particularly close insight into the political circumstances of the late 1570s. The Wars of Religion had a significant role in the renewal of negotiations and both England and France would have much to gain from this match. They also offer a lens into exploring the nature of Elizabethan society as a state, and the polity of the state. Though much has been revealed and discussed from Elizabeth's letters to Anjou, whether it be the political exploitation of marriage negotiations on the queen's part, or her use of a 'courtly love' language to suit this political agenda, there has been little attention paid to the very real affection behind the political in these letters. Though there is much room for discussion in terms of her commitment to the match and to Anjou personally, it is an area of her life that has generally been avoided. This is possibly due to the modern historiographical interpretation of her as an almost-genderless, iconic, virginal, goddess-like ruler, otherwise known as 'Gloriana'.

Though these interpretations can be attributed to Elizabeth in differing contexts, it must be remembered that she was mortal, and as we know from reports of her character, letters, and poetry, the virgin queen was not without emotion. In fact, she was a deeply emotional person who formed real attachments to the people around her, from her beloved Kat, Lord Burghley, to her sweet Robin. The queen had many close attendants who were related to her in some way. It is also known that, because she was rarely alone and constantly surrounded by her ladies, advisors, or courtiers, the formation of close bonds was inevitable. So, if it is well known that she had her favourites, showed real affection for those close to her, and was willing to seriously entertain the prospect of marrying Anjou for the good of her realm (at the beginning of negotiations, at least), then why does it remain so difficult to approach the possibility that she may have felt emotionally tied to him, and may have even borne true affection for the only man she openly and officially courted?

The answer to the question of her true feelings for Anjou is hard to come by. This is because, though we have copies of her letters to him just before and during their courtship, what they say may not necessarily convey what the queen actually meant in her heart. This is most likely why they have been regarded as a political ploy on her part to keep his interest in the idea of a marriage for as long as she could. However, this is only one interpretation based on these letters, which are constructed in such a way that they ooze romance and affection. So, what if, instead of dismissing their language or using them to suit the narrative of Elizabeth as a politically shrewd woman – using men's apparent affections and interests to her advantage – we consider that she may have had some real affection for Anjou?

Though it is obvious that the marriage negotiations between them began as an attempt to form a political alliance that would suit both parties in their endeavour to defeat Spanish influence, exploring the contents of her letters to him, and his reported response, when available, offers a broader view of her feelings and motivations towards her 'frog prince'. Susan Doran has offered a somewhat approachable solution to the question of Elizabeth's motivations behind this match, regarding her commitment as genuine but prevented from going further by the overbearing opinions of her council. Doran suggests the queen's commitment to the match could also have been a policy-making strategy (she is not wrong in this interpretation in terms of the relationship with matrimony and dynastic alliances).[1] But, again, it is only one interpretation and it suits the narrative of a well-researched and creatively structured argument. It must be remembered, however, that many historians are not looking for any hint of love or affection between Elizabeth and Anjou, simply because it does not suit the existing narrative that she was opposed to marriage.

Some have argued that the queen used the 'cult of courtly love' to her advantage, not only in the many marital negotiations throughout her reign but also with some of her closest allies to keep them sweet. Lisa Hilton has suggested that Elizabeth consciously appropriated the same methods of courtly love applied by her mother, Anne Boleyn, whose downfall has often been depicted as her own doing and error, despite the evidence to suggest otherwise. Hilton continues that these tactics were taken up by her, not only as a tool she could use to manipulate foreign policy and her courtiers' minds but as a way of manipulating how her mother's disgrace was interpreted, thus slyly forming a more-glorified image of her mother's memory.[2] Though it is true that Elizabeth applied these courtly love tactics when necessary, it is unlikely that she would have known much of her mother's abilities in this regard, and, as she was a toddler when her mother was executed, it is impossible to imply that use of these practices was an inherited or learned characteristic. It is also important to note that the topic of Anne Boleyn was a tricky one for Elizabeth and her courtiers, and one she often wished to avoid in public. She never outwardly gave her opinion or feelings regarding her mother's downfall and, thus, they are speculative.

It is interesting that her courtship with Anjou in the form of letters came about around the same time she learned of Dudley's secret marriage to Lettice Knollys, Countess of Lennox. This lends to the possibility that she was emotionally vulnerable by the time the beginning of negotiations came about, and rather than typically scolding Burghley and her council of advisors, she felt drawn to the prospect of finding a man to share her bed, her position, and the remainder of her life with. As time went on, and with the eventual arrival of Anjou on English soil, the few letters between them created a platform of familiarity which would have allowed them to ease into a genuinely enjoyable courtship.

We don't know of every conversation or letter between the pair but we do know they became very close. As Tracy Borman has pointed out, this is most likely because Anjou was willing to openly court the ageing queen, and he was also her only foreign suitor to officially court her in person.[3]

Guillaume Coatalen and Jonathan Gibson have analyzed the existing letters of Elizabeth's reign, with particular attention to those regarding foreign policy and, thus, her letters to Anjou. What they have found, transcribed, and interpreted from these letters adds much to the discussion of her negotiations with the duke. What they say about her feelings and their mutual affection and respect is also surprisingly telling. The correspondence in these letters took place between 1578, at the beginning of the second wave of marriage negotiations, and 1584 – the duke's last year alive.[4] Though their courtship would end with no wedding, it is a testimony to the true nature of their affection and mutual respect for one another that they continued their correspondence at all.

Six holograph letters in French from the queen to the duke still exist. These letters, received by Anjou, which in original form were written by Elizabeth's own hand, have survived as part of Lord Burghley's archive in the Cecil Papers at Hatfield House in Hertfordshire. Though they are most likely copied versions, it must be noted that they are probably not altered in content, as her marriage and private life was a concern to the men around her. But what of the duke's feelings? Copies of his letters of response can also be found in the second volume of the Cecil Papers. They were published in 1888 but are now digitized online for the public to read.[5] One letter written by the duke on 2nd March 1579, shows his impatience to meet Elizabeth. He asks her to forgive him for the lateness in the proceedings and blames his brother, the French King, going on to ask her to give Simier the credit for the negotiations.[6] In another letter, written days later, he laments the reports of Elizabeth's subjects' dissatisfaction with the proposed match, due to his religion.[7]

At this stage, leading up to their first meeting, it is difficult to obtain any real affection from his letters, other than his genuine eagerness to settle the negotiations.

The six existing holograph letters written by Elizabeth to Anjou reveal much more than a romantic tone. They are carefully produced, with every detail, whether romantic or political, considered. It is important to note that the letters in their current form are not the versions that reached Anjou. This is because Elizabeth was meticulous in her replies, wanting to address every issue, political and romantic. It is also clear from these practice versions that she was under enormous pressure from her council and subjects in opposition to the match, as she continuously reveals the conflict within herself regarding the issue. These responses are unique in terms of her replies to suitors. Though she was often indecisive in many situations, her swift replies and reactions to her suitors' letters and past negotiations show that her ambivalence during her courtship with Anjou was far more complicated, like that of a political alliance.[8]

In the first holograph letter, she expresses her indecisive nature immediately. She agonized for some days on the granting of Anjou's passport that would allow him to gain safe passage to England to court her in person. Though this letter demonstrates the pressures she was under, it could also reveal a rush of anxiety for her in anticipation of his arrival. Here was a man, some twenty years her junior, requesting passage to England to court her. There was also the question of the succession that possibly weighed on her mind. She was by this time beyond middle-age, and though her physicians stated that she was capable of bearing children, the results of their examinations must be taken with a pinch of salt. Could she still provide England, and France, with an heir? What would this mean for England? It is unsurprising to find that she was anxious for more reasons than the opposition of her council. She was, after all, the queen.

In his letter from 24th June 1579, Mendoza mentions that Elizabeth's reported talents and beauty had attracted Anjou so far as to lead him on his campaign to England to meet the queen in person, without any real reassurance that she would commit to the marriage. Elizabeth's letters in French to the duke are extremely difficult to transcribe. However, in *Elizabeth I's Correspondence: Letters, Rhetoric and politics* by Bajetta, Coatalen, and Gibson, the transcriptions are made as clear as possible, with notes on language, origin, and meaning. The analysis of these letters allows for a deeper insight into the possible affection she had for Anjou, though her indecisive nature is also mentioned. In the first letter, which was sent on 7th July, the queen expresses her wish that Anjou travels to England with safe conduct. However, she begins by expressing her anxieties over her lack of confidence in the proposed match. She also mentions that she has been plagued by the decision of granting the duke's safe passage. It is clear that she was nervous that he would grow weary and frustrated with her indecisive nature and her hesitation to give a direct answer regarding marriage:

> O Monsieur, the trouble which has taken hold of my fancy, wrapped in so much pain, forces me to beg you to weigh well what the end and sequel of this voyage might bring to pass for you — contentment or heart-breaking sorrow — if the business does not conclude in marriage. How cursed I have been since the granting of the passport by the thought that my hand might bring you some disaster or dishonour. You cannot imagine the least part of my sufferings. All I do is dream, wishing more than life itself to assure myself perpetually that neither your good graces nor your peerless affection for me will diminish, whatever the outcome of this matter.[9]

Clearly, she was feeling the mounting pressure from her council, who had always pushed the idea of marriage on her. Now that she had found a man she was willing to consider, her competence was doubted and her sweet Robin had left in a huff. Yet, her letter also reveals that she was in many ways content with the prospect of marrying Anjou. Her use of courtly loving language indicates that she was impatient for his arrival, stating that she hopes her indecisive nature has not dashed his plans to sail to England. Her use of romantic language is not out of the ordinary in terms of sixteenth-century English courtship. She practically re-invented the courtly cult of love, begun during her father's reign, to suit her own political agenda in the past. Yet, this letter seems much different in contrast to that sent to Eric of Sweden.

She continues that she worries about her honour and the discretion of Anjou's proposed visit, explaining that she is devoted to the duke's happiness, whatever the outcome of his visit, and that she fears the consequences if the match should not take place. Though it may seem that she wishes to be as honest as possible in this letter in terms of the possibilities of an advantageous outcome, her genuineness is also clear by her use of language and affectionate referral to the duke as 'my dearest'. It could be argued that her anxieties got the better of her in this letter. We cannot be sure that the contents of this holograph match that of the letter dispatched to Anjou but her attempts to practice her letters and choose her words wisely indicate her intentions to commit to the match where possible. Anjou's 'heart-breaking sorrow', which she mentions at the beginning of the letter, seems a genuine concern for her. It is difficult to conclude from this first letter, whether her expressed feelings about her wish to please Anjou in his pursuit of marriage were genuine or simulated to suit a political agenda. If we are to believe the contents, whether it was for practice or not, we must reconsider what motivated the queen in regards to this match. Historians have been unsure as to whether she was truthful in her apparent intentions to wed Anjou. However, it would be difficult from this one letter to ascertain her feelings, considering that, at this point, she was clearly indecisive about the match and had not yet met the duke. It would seem that Simier's attempts to woo the queen on behalf of Anjou had only half-succeeded. Yet, he did enough for her to grant the duke's passage to England.[10]

The day after she allowed safe conduct for the duke and had the official letter dispatched, her ambassador in France received another packet of letters. It contained a draft for another missive to Anjou that was meant to be sent, yet it remains a part of the archival collection at Hatfield. Here, Elizabeth asks the duke for any further requests he may have regarding his safe conduct and passport. She herself then apologizes for the delay in his trip. There is a reply to this short letter in which he expresses his thanks for safe passage and his sorrow for the delay in his departure, stating that he has no greater desire in the world than to embark on his trip to England.[11]

Regardless of this, he set sail and arrived in England on 17th August 1579, but his presence was to be a secret until Elizabeth wished to welcome him publicly. Why did she want to meet him in secret? Was this a tactic? It most likely was the case that she wished to make sure he was everything Simier boasted of, and she probably wanted to evaluate his character herself to see if there was a possibility of any chemistry between them. Anjou arrived early in the morning – so early that he went to Simier and woke him. He wanted to begin courting the queen straight away, yet Simier convinced him to take respite, then wrote to Elizabeth, telling her of Anjou's arrival and that he wished 'to God you were with him there as he could then with greater ease convey his thoughts to you'.[12]

A letter written by the duke two days after his arrival in England on 19th August, outlines his impatience to be in the company of the queen. He wrote of his affection for her, adding that if she would grant him an audience, he had no doubt that he would satisfy all her scruples. Elizabeth was evidently anxious now that he had actually landed on English soil. But in this letter, it seems that Anjou had a way with words, and encouraged Elizabeth to trust in herself – likely meaning her own feelings and desires.[13]

When they did meet, she seemed immediately taken with him and easily succumbed to his charms. She showered him with gifts and was openly affectionate, to the extent that she gave him the nickname 'my frog'. Anjou also seemed genuinely interested, despite their age difference. He presented her with a diamond worth the sum of 5,000 crowns and stated it was proof of his 'love and goodwill'. The giving of gifts continued, as did the showering of charming compliments, and it seems as though the queen was enjoying his company.[14] Judging by her later letters, the anxiety and language in her first missive, and the reports of their obvious affection during the duke's visit, it can be suggested that their mutual attraction to one another was very real. And, again, though the duke was reportedly scarred from smallpox and suffered a spinal deformity, the ageing queen, also somewhat scarred from her bout of smallpox many years before, seemed happy for the attentions of a young prince. Their letters continued throughout his stay, and, indeed, his use of language to describe his affection for her is evidently similar to hers. In almost every letter, he made sure to remind her of his affection for her.

It must be noted that they both had much to offer in terms of companionship, good conversation, and wit. They were well-educated, shared a similar charm, and each welcomed the other's attentions. It must also be added that both were not born to be the heir-apparent to their respective father's throne, yet Elizabeth was queen and the duke was the Valois heir, as well as Prince of the Netherlands. So, why is it often incomprehensible to many historians that their apparent affections for one another were genuine? They had much in common, and both were in need of an heir, a partner in power, and an ally against Spain. The mutual attraction of both queen and suitor not only added to this courtship but the evidence, in terms of true affection, indicates that there is more to this story than previously believed. This ultimately challenges the existing historiography surrounding Elizabeth's feelings about marriage, and undermines many interpretations of her reign. The other letters written by her to Anjou can add further weight to the theory that perhaps they may have genuinely fallen in love, despite the eventual end of their courtship.

Elizabeth was not ignorant of the grumblings of her council, courtiers, and favourites. She was also aware of her deeper feelings in relation to what was happening in her life. It has been speculated that her true emotional state was down to a number of factors. Firstly, she was aware of her age. Though she was a queen and the daughter of a king, she was not immortal, and what we know as her biological clock was ticking away at the back of her mind. She must have been worried about the succession, especially considering Mary, Queen of Scots' success in producing a male heir in 1566. Susan Doran suspects this to be the case, along with the fact that Dudley had secretly married Lettice Knollys and subsequently taken to his house due to his rage over Anjou's arrival. She also suggests that Anjou could have been a rebound for Elizabeth's emotional trauma from Dudley's betrayal. However, it seems more likely that the queen was in control of her emotions, and Anjou's visit had simply coincided with the rift between Dudley and her.[15] She had known of his secret marriage prior to negotiating Anjou's clandestine visit, and by the time she dispatched the letter on 7th July, she had most likely cooled down, with Dudley already back by her side. It is possible that she was finding it difficult to come to terms with her own feelings, as mentioned in another letter to Anjou, where she states it was difficult – '…in these times to know the difference between seeing and being'.[16]

If she was struggling with the comfort she found in Anjou, she would not have openly made it known. Indeed, she seemed to bask in his attention. She also made every effort to ensure her suitor was comfortable, perhaps even felt at home. The queen and her 'frog' were practically inseparable during his visit and, as he was received at Richmond Palace, where she was born, she presented him with the very bed she was born in. Tracy Borman mentions this act, which was certainly romantic for the period. This gesture, and the fact that Elizabeth personally supervised the furnishing of the duke's rooms, may indicate her serious consideration of this match.[17]

The thought of Elizabeth – the virgin queen and anointed monarch – allowing a suitor to sleep in the bed in which she was born cannot be ignored as an important detail. It says a lot about her initial intentions to show Anjou that she was serious about the prospect of their marriage. It also reflects her sentiments in her first letter sent to him in which she hopes to remain in his good graces, despite delays in his passport's arrival. What is even more surprising is that she jokingly teased him that 'he might recognise the bed'. This mischievous comment has often led others to theorize that she was indicating that she and the duke had shared the same bed the previous evening. However, this has been completely taken out of context, and it must be remembered that, as the queen was never alone, sleeping with her young suitor in the very bed she was born in would not only have been impossible to do in secret and keep as such, it would also have been an unthinkable action for her. The already-existing scandals that surrounded her past relationship with Dudley and her traumatizing stay with Seymour as a young woman must also be considered. It is more likely that she was referring to the fact that this bed was once a part of a ransom paid for a former Duke of Alençon.[18]

During his stay, Anjou remained mostly hidden, though it was probably the worst-kept secret in England. At one stage, he attended a court ball in which he was hidden behind an arras. The queen reportedly tried to conceal her knowledge of his presence but, as she danced, she made a number of gestures towards him, which her courtiers pretended to ignore. Certainly, the presence of a young French prince in suit of the hand of the queen was never going to be easy to conceal. Again, their letters continued to go back and forth, and he stayed in England for ten days, only leaving due to reports of the death of one of his close friends. Yet, it was long enough to make a good impression on Elizabeth.[19] His visit was successful, and the queen's affection for him was clear. Letters written by him from Dover on 29th August and 30th, before he set sail back to France, show his attempts to seduce her with romantic language, whereby he states that 'he will ever remain le plus fidelle et affectionne esclave qui puyse aytre sur la terre' – the most faithful and affectionate slave who could be on earth. He also stated that as soon as he had embarked for France, he would send her back her 'singe' or 'monkey', referring to Simier.[20] Another letter written by him, dated 30th August, is a continuation of his adoration for her. Here he stated that 'since his eyes may no longer behold her whom he adores, nor his words reach her ears, is compelled to have recourse to his pen, which on all possible occasions shall assure her of his fidelity'.[21]

When he returned to France, they kept in contact through letters and exchanged gifts. In January of 1580, she wrote a letter addressing him as her 'dearest' yet again and was sure to convince him of her deep affection for him despite gossip and the opposition of many courtiers and members of her council. The fact that she wished to reassure him in her own hand says much about her true feelings, showing that it was not simply a tactic to dangle France and Spain in a bid to secure England's political influence and safety. This was much more. In the letter, she even complained to him about Dudley's opposition to the match and general arrogance towards her newfound happiness:

> those who make the people believe that you are so arrogant and so inconstant that they can easily make us withdraw our favour from our dearest when they have us to themselves.[22]

Her affections are also obvious through her humour. She seemed to be quite playful in her letters to him. The language of courtly love is easily detectable through the softness of this letter and the ease in her jokes and playfulness. She jested that she would give a million pounds to see her frog swimming in the Thames again.[23] Though this may seem insulting considering the duke's deformities, it shows a more relaxed atmosphere between them, indicating that they were by this stage very comfortable in how they expressed their feelings to one another.

While the majority of historians agree that Elizabeth thoroughly enjoyed most of her courtships, as it fed her vanity, the debate over her sincerity towards them continues. Some believe that her feelings for Anjou do not matter in terms of understanding the larger picture. However, to gain a true representation of who she was or, rather, who she became, we must consider every aspect of her nature, character, and, when possible, her personal feelings. It may seem a difficult task to pull her true sentiments and motivations from a letter that also suited a political agenda as well as a personal one but if we interpret these hints of affection as genuine rather than flattery, we gain a well-rounded version of her as the woman, rather than simply Elizabeth the queen. Though she clearly enjoyed her courtship with the duke, we cannot dismiss her serious intentions to marry, as Levin points out.[24]

The fact that she approached the opportunity for re-opening marriage negotiations with Anjou, and permitted him to attend her court, though in secret, clearly indicates her intention to consider the possibility of marriage. It also seems that she wanted it to follow through. Some believe that this suggests her emotional connection to and genuine feelings for him. And, yet, the winning argument is often that she was merely scheming with the intention of securing a favourable foreign policy.[25] Perhaps the truth may lie somewhere in the middle of these two theories. Again, there is no doubt that she began the negotiations, yet again, in pursuit of a strong political alliance. But somewhere along the way, her emotions took hold and she became enthralled in her courtship. Whether this was because it made her feel young or beautiful does not matter. The fact that she expressed her feelings for Anjou so flamboyantly, something she had never done for any other man, possibly even Dudley, says a lot more about her character as a woman, rather than a monarch. Could this interpretation of her be more reasonable or realistic?

Her familiarity with Anjou in her letters could reveal her true affections for him. These are not her typical replies to a foreign, princely suitor. Indeed, they are much more interesting. Her language in comparison to that of letters to Eric of Sweden, for example, are decorative, almost poetic, and symbolic of her desires to make Anjou her husband. In one letter dated 17th March 1581, she again opened with 'my dearest', which is something she did only in her writings to him. She thanks him for the token of flowers which he sent to her. Yet, it is the language used rather than the gesture of thanks that should be noted. The familiarity is unquestionable, and, thus, their mutual affections undeniable:

> Thanking you humbly for the sweet flowers culled by the hand that has the little fingers that I bless a million times.[26]

The language used here expresses intimacy. If her feelings were not reciprocated by the duke, it would be surprising. This is because the phrase 'little fingers' may not seem exactly affectionate out of context but, rather, a mockery. However, because the queen may have written this knowing that it would be received well by the duke, it indicates that they perhaps shared an intimate joke or that, simply, she found beauty where others were repulsed. It could be assumed that he wasn't offended by her affectionate remarks and was likely charmed by her familiarity, seeing as there is no evidence of it in his letters to her.

By examining the existing letters and notes from Elizabeth to him, overlooking that they were unfinished versions and not dispatched, the idea that she fell in love with him during his visit to England is not as far-fetched as has been previously believed. Many have argued that she deeply loved Dudley, and though it is true that she most likely was once in love with him, she was always careful not to entertain his suit for marriage, going so far as to express that she could never marry him – for reasons we already know. However, her draft letters for Anjou reveal an even more-realistic interpretation of her feelings for the Anglo-French courtship. They are somewhat frantic, emotional, and convey all of her thoughts, anxieties, worries, and hopes in a stream of chaotic and romantic language. Though it is often difficult to translate her letters in French, what can be ascertained offers a great deal of her raw emotion.

Anjou's letters to her after his 'secret visit' suggest his longing for her 'answer' to the question of their marriage. His tone is romantic, and though it allows for great argument in terms of the validity of their affection for each other, he often comes across as rather desperate. He states in a letter dated 10th October 1579, that he hopes 'nostre singe…' – 'your monkey' – evidently referring to Simier again, would bring him [Anjou] some 'favourable resolution'.[27]

It is perhaps better to have the drafts of her letters, rather than the official ones dispatched, as they contain a more serious tone, like some of her later letters to him in 1580 and 1581. Neville Williams argues that Elizabeth had indeed fallen in love with Anjou and that she also probably believed that she could control him and, therefore, have a discreet political influence in his affairs. Williams also states that, if it were entirely up to Elizabeth herself, and she had full control over the negotiations without the advice of her council, the proposal would have been accepted openly and a marriage probably would have taken place. Instead of giving her full heart to the duke, some remained her own and, therefore, England's.[28] We know that, in the end, her heart was overruled by her head, as was usually the case, but it is clear from such excerpts of her early letters to the duke and reports of his visit to England, that she had truly fallen for her frog prince, 'warts', or, rather, pockmarks, and all.

As they continued to correspond over a period of many months, the precarious reality would soon dawn on the queen that her endeavour to marry the duke was not going to come about easily. Despite the many objections of her council, subjects, and favourites, she also had a deep conflict within herself. Religion was one issue that she could perhaps overlook in a private context but the measures of power and the duke's desire for it would also prompt her anxiety. This did not initially cool her desire to marry Anjou but it would ultimately influence her later decisions. Certainly, she wished for her affections to be reciprocated. This is one way of verifying her feelings for him. In her letters, the language she uses is often confusing, yet hints of her affections come through on every line. The queen was put in a state of worry and under enormous pressure by her subjects and council, and later events would prove that she had a lot more to contemplate than her own feelings, which were probably the only factor that convinced her to stand against the opposition that would form around her. In the letter written to Anjou from March of 1581, she writes of her affections for him and the fact that they will not be altered, come any storm. Her words can only be transcribed as a woman in love and a woman with worry:

I content myself, Monsieur, that you assure yourself of me as of most faithful friend that ever prince had. And if you trust to such a rock all the tempests of the sea will be far from shaking it, nor will any storm on the earth turn it aside from honouring and loving you.[29]

It appears that she is acknowledging Anjou's affections for her.

This further implies that, despite the odds against them, they were actually very much in love, or at least had deep affection and respect for one another. Her open double-negative response, though difficult to fully comprehend of its full meaning, is doubly indicative of her recognition of his feelings for her: '...I cannot satisfy it at all, unless I fail to recognize it by all the means that are in my power'.[30] It is clear that she wants further proof of the shared love between them. Therefore, if she was simply using him to suit a political agenda, would she really have gone through so much trouble as to express her wanting of his affection?

Despite their apparent feelings, this would not be enough. As was the case with most royal marriages and courtships, there were much greater concerns than the feelings of those involved. With an overbearing amount of opposition to come, the queen would have to live up to her own words in her letters if she was to stand strong. However, as her intention to marry Anjou became clear, many of her subjects reacted with alarm. Some shuddering instances were to take place that would push this courtship to a point where it could no longer return to its beginnings of mutual affection. Politics and love did not mix well, at least, not in Elizabethan England. On 17th July 1579, Elizabeth was travelling from Greenwich to Deptford by barge when a bullet was shot from a light musket by Thomas Appletree, injuring one of her oarsmen. Appletree was apparently hunting birds along the Thames but the initial implication that this was an assassination attempt would have shaken the queen's nerve, and also enraged her. It was probably assumed that this attempt was due to the presence of her Lord Admiral and also Simier. Later, it was determined that this was an accident on Appletree's part, and so, for a time, life at court returned to normal, as did Elizabeth's affections for the duke. Their letters continued, their affections growing seemingly stronger, but much more opposition was to come. Tears were no longer her only weapon to get what she wanted. This great love would lead to bloodshed.[31]

Chapter 5

A Kingdom in Opposition

Elizabeth did all she could to ensure that her marriage with Anjou would go ahead. However, negotiations were halted after the duke's departure, as her council could not come to a unanimous agreement on the match. Even prior to his arrival in January, any collective agreement seemed impossible. Many who opposed their marriage, protested that the match could be a danger to the stability of the Protestant Religion. By this time, it must have occurred to Elizabeth that this kind of opposition was unavoidable. Some members of her council even expressed their concerns over her own doubts about the match. Yet, her letters to the duke do not indicate any doubt of her feelings for or intentions to marry him. On the contrary, her warnings to him that there would be much opposition, especially after his 'secret' visit, indicate that she was well aware of the many obstacles to her happiness.[1]

However, was this marriage and her pursuit of happiness more important to her than the love of her people and the admiration of her council? If so, wouldn't she have bypassed the advice of the men around her and married Anjou, anyway? As is usually the case, the situation was more complicated than this. If her council opposed the match, and if her subjects followed suit, she risked far more than his love or her chance to secure the Tudor Dynasty – she risked her position and her people's loyalty. The public reaction to the match would have shaken her reserve and made her doubt the possibility of a marriage to Anjou without any consequences. If she did not have the support of her people, then she could easily end up in the same situation as her cousin and rival for the English throne, the dethroned and disgraced Mary, Queen of Scots. Perhaps one of the greatest questions is why her council and subjects couldn't see any room for further negotiations surrounding the sensitive topics of religion and the wielding of power.

It is clear from other letters to the duke that she was beginning to show signs of serious doubt of their courtship ending in marriage. As mentioned before, her comment in one letter in French translates roughly as '…in these times to know the difference between seeming and being.' This indicates that her indecisive nature was surfacing once again. But is this all that can be taken from this small quote? It could also suggest that what she really felt was not what mattered to those around her. So, though she seemed to be in love – and it is doubtful that she had no affection for the duke – who she was as a woman or how she felt simply didn't matter. If her council could not fully support the idea of the marriage, and if she didn't even have the support of her loving subjects, then how could she enter into a marriage with Anjou, regardless of their mutual affection? Much had changed since the reign of her father.

The negotiations added fuel to the already burning anti-Catholic sentiment throughout the kingdom, and the response was definitive. Not only did the open hostility of the people worry the queen, her council's inability to come to a conclusion infuriated her. It is also probably the case that the remarks of her council and the reaction of her people on paper, had a serious effect on her emotional state. When faced with widespread hostility and opposition to something that had become much more than a political alliance, it is not surprising that she would eventually crumble. But it is also clear that she was still working towards some form of negotiation with her council that would allow the marriage to take place.[2]

It is clear that she was not only undecided but also extremely impatient for an indication that a marriage to Anjou would be wholly approved by her council. However, on 7th October, a message was presented to her indicating that though they were sorry for the delay in a decision, they wished for her to 'shew to them any inclination of her mind, they will so proceed that her honour shall be preserved and whatsoever may seem burdensome they will bear with common consent...'[3] This implies that though her council were mostly opposed to the match, they accepted the necessity of her marriage for the safety and stability of the realm. Ultimately, it seems that they wished for Elizabeth to dictate her will in the matter but to take heed of their individual opinions and counsel. But this was not what she wanted, and she depended on the guidance of her most trusted advisers.

Lord Burghley had noted the danger of a lack of marriage for the queen and what it meant for the succession and future of England. His papers record the general lack of support Elizabeth and Anjou had but they also show her stubborn nature. This is mentioned on 7th October 1579, where it is noted that the queen:

> never speaketh of him [Anjou] but with great allowance of his nature and conditions; and lastly, she seemeth not pleased with any person or with any argument appearing to mislike of the marriage.[4]

Regardless of the council's inability to come to a conclusion, which would either finalize the marriage negotiations or end them entirely, a treaty was drawn up in November which included a provision that Anjou could practice Catholicism as his conscience dictated, but only after marriage to Elizabeth and only in private. If the queen's council were overall opposed to the marriage, then why would they provide provisions for the duke based on his marriage to her? It seems questionable as to why this wasn't considered before. Simier, the duke's envoy, had remained in England throughout this period, probably by order of Anjou, to employ his charms to keep the queen's interests in the match. He sent the treaty off to France but, crucially, while

Elizabeth agreed to sign the treaty contract, it was on condition that it could be set aside if she could not marry Anjou due to the opposition of her people.[5] Some historians have argued that this could be evidence of her uncertainty over the match and, thus, of her own feelings for the duke. Yet, if she was truly unsure of her feelings for him, would she really have signed her future away to a foreign prince, and evidently on paper? It seems that the only reason for her insistence that the treaty could be disregarded at any time on her terms indicates her fears over her people's reaction to her chosen suitor. Due to her indecisive nature, it is known that she often took her time to sign documents, an example of this being the death warrant of Mary, Queen of Scots.

The deadline here was clear – she had a maximum of two months before a decision would have to be made regarding her proposed marriage. By 20th January 1580, she was clearly under enormous pressure, not helped by the French ambassador stating that if she did not marry the Duke of Anjou, then her letters to him would be publicly published for the world to see, thus revealing her true feelings, and assurances to him. It is evident here that her feelings for him were no secret, and that if the ambassador knew of her promises and confessed affections for the duke, then it is likely that the whole court, and possibly the whole kingdom, knew of her intentions to marry him. This threat not only angered the queen, but it would also have knocked her confidence in the match and in her own feelings for him. She also sought the advice of Burghley, one of the few men who, by this time, she could trust. Interestingly, his response could indicate his understanding of her feelings, and yet the safety and security of the realm were paramount. Indeed, the queen most likely expressed that she could not sacrifice her political and personal independence in this case. Burghley's advice seems to have shocked her. He suggested that she make a decision, stick by it, and then find a way to explain it to Anjou. This was probably the most heartfelt advice she was ever going to get on this matter, considering her other councillors wanted her to keep France dangling for as long as possible.[6]

A second holograph letter exists in which she speaks of the pressures of this deadline. This could be her using Burghley's advice, putting forward an argument against the marriage and, yet, though she also outlines the hostility in England towards the match, it seems more likely that this letter was written to inform Anjou of the difficulties ahead in securing their marriage.[7] Though this version was seemingly never sent, another more formal version was, which indicates the stress on public opposition to Catholicism in any form. Despite the formality in which she often wrote to Anjou, in every letter, there is a hint of sentimentality, familiarity, and true affection. In the sent version of this letter, she confided that there was:

> no prince in the world to whom I would more willingly yield to be his than to yourself, nor with whom I would pass the years of my life.[8]

This is probably one of the most telling of her confessions to the duke, as it indicates that she not only saw in him an equal match in royal blood and status, and a useful foreign alliance, but also a man she could spend the rest of her life with. By this time, she would have been aptly aware of her own mortality, and therefore was eager to find a partner she could enjoy the rest of her days with. She also mentions in this letter to Anjou from January 1580, that she is aware of the hostility towards the match but that she knows of their true feelings as individuals and as a pair:

> I have no doubts about our agreements as individuals, being uncertain as much about not complying as not assured that I should consent.

This indicates that she is trying to inform the duke of the great pressure and strain upon her from her people and council. It also reveals another side to her – the rather 'meek and feeble' woman she so heartedly used to her advantage in the past. It seems that, though she was a Tudor, and the queen, she also was compelled as a female monarch to comply with the council's advice regarding her marriage negotiations, due to the possible consequences of ignoring them. There is plenty of evidence to suggest that she feared the same fate as her cousin Mary, who had some time before reaching out to her for help after entering into a disastrous marriage, which her own advisors and people despised. It is also evident from Mary I's marriage, that a foreign match could bring further rebellion and religious turmoil. This letter shows that Elizabeth is not in fact using Burghley's advice by letting the duke down but, rather, using her familiarity and close bond with Anjou to express her true feelings on the matter:

> And at this hour I would not deceive you by not placing openly before your eyes how I find the case, and what I think of it, in which I have had so much regard to your ease and contentment as if for my own life or consideration of my state, which would otherwise have moved me to make another answer.[9]

It is also clear that by expressing her true feelings in this way, she clearly valued his opinion and sought his advice. Because we do not have his replies, it is difficult to gain a true evaluation of their shared thoughts on the matter. Despite the pressures, their affections for one another did not cool off and the letters kept going back and forth between England and France. Elizabeth speaks of the letters she received from him, which indicates that his replies were as swift and romantically centred as hers. It can only be imagined what his response to the English opposition to the match was. However, her letters have left us with a hint of the duke's affections:

> I see your affection is not diminished by your absence nor cools by persuasions, of which I can only return a sincere and immovable goodwill, ready to serve you on all occasions contrary or ill…[10]

This is very strong language, and though it indicates a romantic side to the courtship, by Elizabeth indicating her readiness to 'serve' the duke, we can see this as her meaning to conduct herself as a dutiful and respectful wife, if not queen. This readiness to serve on any occasion, whether ill or contrary, seems somewhat symbolic of wedding vows. So, if we are to believe that they were really in love, what did others have to say about it? According to Mendoza's records, and the reactions of her council, her subjects were in general opposition to the match. But who were these subjects? A letter from Sir Philip Sidney in 1579 gives a clear indication of the opposition she faced. Here, he attempts to dissuade the queen from marrying Anjou, and the strong language is telling as to why their love could never be.

Elizabeth knew that many of her courtiers and subjects were opposed to the match on the grounds of religion, yet, clearly from her own letters, her view of the matter was that religion mattered little in the affairs of her heart. Sidney's letter to her may have influenced her uncertain position over the match in terms of gaining the support of her subjects, yet it would not ultimately dissuade her from continuing to find a means of getting what she wanted. His language may be strong, considering he was writing to his sovereign, yet his words must have made some resonance, as it is notable that, at this time, he was not knighted and, thus, the referral of him as 'Sir' is due to his knighthood long after this letter was written.

We see that he begins with the typical humble and obedient

tone of a subject to his sovereign: 'Most feared and beloved, most sweet and gracious sovereign.'[11] He continues in an apologetic tone, almost aware that what he will say next might enrage the queen. Truly, it seems from the beginning of his letter that he meant well, considering he already knew that his queen's reaction was going to be volatile. His use of language, though strong, shows his true nature and indicates his bravery to confront the matter. As he states: 'To seek out excuses of this my boldness, and to arm the acknowledging of a fault with reasons for it…', he is excusing his choice of language whilst also defending its purpose and the content of the letter. He also mentions the carrying of 'olive branches', which is an indication of his attempt to make peace prior to fully exposing his argument against her match with Anjou. His motivation, though thoroughly reasoned, would not have given the queen any pleasure nor reassurance in the matter, yet he pushed forth with his argument that Anjou was unsuitable for her, and unprofitable for the realm. He speaks in this first paragraph only of his adoration for the queen and of his hopes that she will be merciful, considering his directness. It ends rather neatly, with him indicating that he is well aware of her possible violent reaction. In stating this, he was not only pardoning himself prior to condemnation but also employing a tactic to make her aware of his fears for her in this matter, and to make her more aware that his opinions mattered, and had to be taken into consideration.[12]

Sidney argues that surely Elizabeth is stronger where she is, meaning unmarried and with personal power. He asks her to consider what may happen to her in terms of her 'state and person', indicating that her position as queen is not only in danger due to the match but, also, as a woman, she is subject to the will of her husband. Elizabeth the woman and Elizabeth the queen could not afford to be separated in this way. Sidney's use of persuasive language is unique. Clearly, he implies that he is an experienced courtier, and the contents of this letter, though controversial, allow for an insight into how she cultivated this unique language in her court. One could openly oppose the sovereign's match but, because of the careful nature of the writing, you could get away with it to an extent. This was a brave move, considering the severity of punishment meted out to others in opposition to the marriage. Sidney states that this match would be hazardous to the queen's person, and, thus, hazardous to the realm. He asks her why she so suddenly has changed her attitude, possibly towards marriage in general, possibly towards Anjou, though this is not made quite clear:

> What maketh you in such a calm to change course, to so healthful a body to apply such a weary medicine?[13]

The symbolism in this question, however, is clear. Elizabeth is the perfect example of a healthy and natural sovereign, born a princess of Tudor blood. So why apply unnecessary changes that may alter her good health? In other words, have an effect on her good status and reputation. Notably, this symbolism carries through where Sidney describes the sinews of her crown as her subjects. Not only does he remind her that her actions and decisions are subject to the will of her people but he ultimately informs her that there is a divide in the reactions to her courtship with Anjou:

> The patient I account your realm; the agent Monsieur, and his design; for neither outward accidents do much prevail against a true inward strength; nor doth inward weakness lightly subvert itself, without being thrust at by some outward force. Your inward force (for as for your treasures indeed, the sinews of your crown, your Majesty doth best and only know) consisteth in your subjects, generally unexpert in warlike defence; and as they are divided now into mighty factions...[14]

This divide, he sums up, is due to the two differing factions where religion is concerned. This is where most of the queen's council could not come to an agreement, based on the difference in religion and the implications of such a match, despite it being beneficial to the Wars of Religion. Sidney also implies throughout this letter the real danger to the queen's person, based on the fact that many of her subjects are Catholic. This, in his mind, would have opened up the possibility of the conspiracy of a Catholic plot and, as Mary, Queen of Scots was by this time still alive and in England, his concerns over Anjou's religion can be taken as genuine. In terms of Elizabeth's Protestant subjects, he is concerned for their loyalty to her, considering her intentions to wed a 'papist'. If we look back to her sister Mary's reign and the great opposition to her marriage to Philip of Spain, it is clear that a Catholic foreign match during a period of great persecution for Protestants would have made any Protestant Englishman uncomfortable, to say the least. Sidney's fears for a rebellion against Elizabeth's sovereignty if she married a Catholic were well-founded, and though it was probably clear to most courtiers by now that the queen was in love, his letter shows the real pressure on her, which she would eventually succumb to.[15]

He was also brave enough to make his view of Anjou clear in this letter. The language may be strong but his concerns seem truly genuine, though perhaps somewhat based on general sentiments of those opposed to the match. It must be considered that others advised him as to what to include in this letter. He states that he believed Anjou to be a character of light mind, his will being 'of light ambition as is possible'. This is, of course, referring to the fact that, though Anjou may feel for Elizabeth as she does for him, his attempts to gain her favour come from greater ambitions. Sidney mentions the duke's attempts against his own brother, and his endeavour to meddle in the situation of the Low Countries are an indication of his true nature. He also mentions that Anjou had been as thoroughly interested in the king of Spain's daughter as he was in Elizabeth.

It is clear that Sidney was willing to make his opposition to the match personal as well as political. His argument was to attract Elizabeth's attention, and the mention of Anjou's possible affections for another, perhaps younger, royal woman, would have certainly done that. Whether she believed this is unknown. Cleverly, he also mentions that if Anjou cannot seem to find contentment by being the heir of France and, therefore, the second most important man in the country, then what would that imply if he was to sit beside Elizabeth on the throne, second to that of a woman? 'Since…he that cannot be content to be second person in France and heir apparent would come to be the second person where he should pretend no way sovereignty.'[16] Also, would Anjou be able to keep within the limits of Elizabeth's conditions? Sidney considers this, and believes that the duke's inability to be content with his position in France is proof of that.

His argument certainly gives food for thought, and though the eventual end to the match would cause her great distress, even heartbreak, it was, overall, perhaps best for the final years of her reign and the stability of her realm.[17] This letter is shrewd, yet Sidney clearly outlines that his concern is for Elizabeth's well-being and her 'estate', which is referring to her person as much as her kingdom, wealth, and personal power. There seems to have been a real fear on behalf of her subjects that if she married Anjou, he would be king. The possibility of him gaining substantial power was very real and, in this case, Sidney expresses that such a shift in power would do more harm to the realm than it would benefit it:

And if he grow King, his defense will be like Ajax's shield, which weighed down rather than defended those that bare it.[18]

He also includes some praise for the queen in her work as protector of God's Church in England. His insistence that her ability to do this alone is sufficient evidence that she should continue to do so. This is also an indication of his worries about Anjou's Catholicism. His mention that the duke's 'profession' in Catholicism could not in any way 'stead'[19] the queen's cause for the Protestant Church in England. Towards the ending of the letter, the language becomes much less insistent and directive, as if, after vomiting his worries and concerns as a man, he is once again rendered the humble subject. In the final paragraph, he asks Elizabeth to trust in the advice of her subjects and particularly her council, who has advised her throughout her many years on the throne: 'Let those whom you find trust, and to whom you have committed trust in your weighty affairs, be held up in the eyes of your subjects.'[20] The last sentence of his letter may well be an attempt to smooth over his attempts throughout to direct her decisions and to tactically use his impression of Anjou to channel her mood: 'Lastly, doing as you do, you shall be as you be: the example of princesses, the ornament of your age, the comfort of the afflicted, the delight of your people, the most excellent fruit of your progenitors, and the perfect mirror of your prosperity.'[21]

Though his language is shrewd, it cannot be concluded whether the queen would have found this infuriating or amusing. Certainly, this letter would not have pleased her, and, yet, despite her feelings for Anjou and his apparent return of those affections, she would have by this time known that the advice of her council could no longer be ignored and that the sentiments expressed by Sidney were that of her kingdom, not as a whole but by majority, nonetheless. If this letter was to shock her and make her question herself, there was more to come. Her closest advisor and confidant, Burghley, was penning his own petition to her as this letter from Sidney was sent. But Sidney and Burghley were not the only subjects of Elizabeth's to openly make their opinions of the proposed marriage plain. Several London preachers, who probably had the advice and encouragement of the queen's own council and other distinguished members of the Protestant elite, voiced their concerns for what they felt would be an 'ungodly union'.[22] This would have only prompted further opposition to the match. It began prior to Sidney's letter, and while Elizabeth responded to critics of the match with great anger and outrage, her mood and sentiments on the matter would have been further affected by this missive.

It seems that Sidney got off rather lightly in comparison to earlier opponents to the match. This may well be because of his position as a courtier or some favour the queen had for him. As he felt capable of producing and sending such a letter to her, it could be suggested that he knew it may cause offence, even outrage, but not enough to land him in hot enough waters to threaten his life and position. A Member of Parliament, and pamphleteer, Thomas Norton, was sent to the Tower after making a speech openly condemning the queen's endeavours to marry Anjou. John Stubbs also previously faced horrific treatment due to his open hostility to the idea of a French-Catholic match. He was a well-known lawyer and author, with deep connections with Elizabeth's court, as well as factions of radical Protestants, and penned *The discoverie of a gaping gulf whereinto is like to be swallowed by another French marriage...*, showing open hostility to the queen's agenda and, as Richards sums up quite precisely, was 'a comprehensive assault on the whole idea of the marriage'.[23] If such material was capable of floating around court and making its way across her kingdom, Elizabeth had no chance of securing the marriage with Anjou, and, thus, had no chance of true happiness in her later life.

Sidney was careful in terms of the language he used to describe his opposition to any marriage between the queen and Anjou but Stubbs shows his unfamiliarity with her wrath, and his inability to restrain his argumentative nature and inexperience as a shrewd courtier. 1579 seems to have been a strenuous year for Elizabeth, not only because of the ongoing turmoil in Europe, which saw her many Protestant brothers and sisters slaughtered and her indecisiveness over her marriage negotiations, but the pressure from her councillors in regards to her reactions and actions towards both. Stubbs' publication and circulation of *The Discoverie of a Gaping Gulf* would not have eased her strain, nor her temper. The way in which he describes not only the French but Anjou himself and his apparent agenda, would have insulted her intelligence, and her integrity. His argument clearly indicates a disdain for the French in general and his overt hatred for the Roman Catholic religion, which was the main element for his opposition to Elizabeth's betrothal. Perhaps what is most shocking about this pamphlet is that Stubbs openly questioned the queen's judgment of character and her commitment to the Protestant faith. Her reaction, therefore, is unsurprising, and was seemly necessary considering the delicate position of the Protestant faith at the time.

In his protest, Stubbs, unlike Sidney, refrains from excusing his language anywhere in his text, and though this document is not a letter and therefore not addressed to the queen personally, he would not have been in any doubt that the queen would eventually read it, and therefore his inability to think strategically as a courtier is obvious. Not that he would have wanted to. He first mentions the 'heathens' are blind to 'a certain divine nature'. These words are indicative of those he believed 'unknown to God', who he refers to as 'papists' or Catholics. In the beginning, it is clear that his main argument would be based on religion. The man's loathing for the French is evident, and therefore his later interpretation of Anjou can only offer a one-sided view of the duke as a person. His initial referral to the French implies that he has already made up his mind on Anjou and the marriage negotiations. Also, his view of the French, in general, is telling:

This sickness of mind have the French drawn from those eastern parts of the world as they did that other horrible disease of the body and having already too far westward communicated the one contagion, do now seek notably to infect our minds of the other.[24]

The 'horrible disease of the body' Stubbs is referring to is now known as Syphilis, yet many an Englishman during this period would have referred to it as 'The French Disease', so Stubbs' view in this was not uncommon. On Anjou, in particular, he refers to him as an 'imp' and 'the old serpent in shape of a man', whose true endeavour is to seduce Elizabeth, whom he refers to as their 'Eve' and a 'Lordly Lady'. This description of his queen may have been an attempt to make up for his description of Anjou as evil itself, yet it is doubtful it made any difference. He conveys his fears that, through Anjou, the papacy will undermine Elizabeth and therefore threaten 'the foundations of our commonwealth'. Also, he openly asks that the queen does not grant the duke to hear daily Mass. This is most likely in fear that it would further encourage Catholic Mass and threaten the queen's position.[25]

Stubbs' anxiety is clear at the prospect of the French governing England through Elizabeth if she were to marry Anjou, and though this was a true and valid fear for the council in general, and perhaps even the queen, it is unlikely that she would have gone ahead with negotiations knowing that such an outcome may have been the case. The mention of 'this dangerous practice of marriage' which 'wrappeth Queen Elizabeth in her lifetime and her England together alike', shows the strain she experienced to marry and then to not marry was well known. The emotional and psychological effect this had on her has yet to be examined. It is inarguable that opposition to this match was based on the duke being French and Catholic but the judgment of him expressed in this document was by this time based on more than him or the French alone – it was a judgement of Elizabeth's character. Stubbs ends his argument stating that he simply fears for the queen's reign and life, and that she should reconsider the marriage. He hints that he does not wish to offend her with his argument, and speaks openly of his affections for her. However, he did not have the ability to manipulate his words to pardon his argument, as Sidney would later do.[26]

Elizabeth's first reaction to his open hostility (for all to see) was to have him and his two accomplices hanged. Much like her father, she was incapable of rational decisions when angry, but was dissuaded from this harsh punishment and the matter went before a jury. This was most likely on the advice of Burghley, as the outcome could not then be directly blamed on her. That September, it was decided that Stubbs and a 'major distributor' of the pamphlet should each have their right hand cut off. Interestingly, the printer of the material was excused from any punishment due to his 'old age'. Reports stated that it took 'three blows' to remove Stubbs' hand from his arm. However, a surgeon was permitted to be present so the perpetrators did not bleed to death. Stubbs would spend another year locked up in the Tower before being released. What is most telling about Elizabeth's reaction to Stubbs' pamphlet is not the punishment given but the proclamation that followed, which condemned his work and openly defended Anjou. As Richards mentions, this was most likely a tactic to gain her subjects' approval for the match. Her attempts, however, would lead nowhere.[27]

Richards also mentions that the queen's response to these events reveals her feelings for Anjou. Yet, ultimately, any argument that her response to this pamphlet was due to her own judgement without the advice of her council is unfounded. It is also most likely that Stubbs' argument, like Sidney's, was fueled by Elizabeth's own council and, thus, their betrayal of her in a way must be considered. The council's reaction towards Stubbs' publication is also unusual. Though they were most likely glad of its circulation, they also condemned it in front of the queen. Their agreement on the punishment is also unusual, as they were well aware of the Spanish threat due to their landing in the South-West of Ireland to stir Catholic rebellion against England. This was a complicated situation, which Elizabeth nor her council were fully prepared for. They needed France as an ally to counter Spain, yet they could never accept the idea of the queen marrying Anjou. Both situations threatened the Protestant religion and Elizabeth's reign but only one threatened any possible future with the duke.[28]

Stubbs' argument in comparison to Sidney's was far less diplomatic, and his punishment is evidence of that. However, the language expressed by Stubbs and Sidney, and later by Burghley, indicates that, as a whole, Elizabeth had most of her subjects against her in the affairs of her heart. Though Burghley would come to support his queen in her endeavour to marry Anjou, the open hostility towards the match says a lot for the actual amount of diplomatic power she held as monarch. Sidney's letter looks to have been almost thrust upon him, and it seems it was encouraged by the militant Protestant factions at court. This most likely explains his tactics and careful use of language, as opposed to Stubbs, who most definitely decided to pen his work himself based on his own deep-seethed opposition to the match and hatred of the French. The Earl of Leicester, and the queen's spymaster, Walsingham, were also openly hostile to the match but, like Sidney, they were careful. Sidney's punishment, too, or the lack of it, is also indicative of his family's important position at court, which was a necessary position. His letter wasn't published in his own lifetime and, thus, did not circulate around court as Stubbs' pamphlet did.

Philip Sidney retired to his sister's property in the countryside sometime between 1579 and 1580 and did not continue in his position at court. It is possible that the queen sent him away because of his letter and opposition to the match but it isn't clear whether this was actually the case. There were other reasons for him to retreat from court and retire to a more solitary life, such as his falling out with the Earl of Oxford, who was a favourite of the queen. Therefore, a hasty retirement to the country would have been in his best interest considering his letter was sent to the queen around the same time as his quarrel with Oxford.[29] Every copy of Stubbs' pamphlet they found was confiscated to prevent further ruin to the prospect of Elizabeth and Anjou marrying. The possession of the publication was prohibited and people were informed to avoid speaking of it, including the clergy in their sermons, regardless of their opinions. However, the damage was done and, in printing his opposition to the match, Stubbs opened the door for more opposition. The puritan movement was also growing in England, and a ballad expressed their feelings of the match:

> The King of France Shall not advance his ships in English sand.
> Nor shall his brother Francis have the ruling of the land:
> We subjects true unto our Queen the foreign yoke defy.
> Whereto we plight our faithful hearts, our limbs, our lives and all.
> Thereby to have our honour rise, or take our fatal fall.
> Therefore, good Francis, ruler at home, resist not our desire;
> For here is nothing else for thee, but only sword and fire.[30]

In the aftermath of Stubbs' very public punishment and Sidney's somewhat arguable disgrace following their penned/printed opposition to Elizabeth and Anjou's matter, Lord Burghley was also contemplating his own thoughts on the queen's desires and how to express them. His character has always been something of a paradox to historians in this matter. He wanted to give Elizabeth what she wanted but he also knew what England needed and what it could do without. It seems that he was somewhat sympathetic to her feelings for Anjou. When reading her letters, drafts or not, it is clear that she felt passionately for the duke. Indeed, the fact that Burghley wished to please her, where possible, is perhaps more telling than her own letters.

It would seem that Elizabeth had few people on her side in this matter. Perhaps Burghley was the only person close to her who genuinely supported the French match. Whether this is because he knew of her affections for Anjou or felt that the match would allow for some seriously favourable political advantages, is open to speculation. However, the latter seems more realistic. On the political front, he most likely felt that, in matrimony, France was an affordable and necessary ally, and he pressed Elizabeth on the issue from an all-political stance, rather than that of the romantic. In his view, the match would be contrary to Stubbs and Sidney's arguments, benefiting the Protestant cause, not hindering it. Spain's political stance would be altered, the Netherlands would be secure, and England would be safe and no longer alone in Europe.[31]

Interestingly, his most well-known support for Elizabeth and Anjou's match in his letter, written personally for the queen, barely mentions the political, if only for pragmatic reasons. Here, he was more concerned for her personal welfare and happiness. It is clear that his language is more natural, less formal, and more familiar in regards to how he addresses her and how he chooses to explain his views. He may well be on her side, as it were, but he was still conscious of her being his sovereign and better, regardless of her gender. This says a lot about Elizabeth's relationship with him, almost as much as it says about her relationship with Anjou. Burghley's mention that the ageing queen was in need of 'some partner' to give her 'delight, honour', and, most interestingly, 'pleasure', shows that the queen's favourite councillor was not ignorant to her needs as a woman. Historians now should not ignore the fact that she was, behind it all, a woman, who, by this time in her life, was in much need of a partner in life for comfort, enjoyment, and even pleasure. Burghley asks the queen to 'tarry' a little in her impatience for the council's answer regarding her marriage.[32]

It would seem that he was, in some way, convinced that her will would eventually come to fruition. In relation to her own pleasure, he is careful in how he writes. His words are almost poetic, and within them lies a serious note on the queen's deserving of a partner, considering her years of service and her subjects' love. However, he also mentions that, though she may love Anjou—'...lives the man and speaks he English that you highly esteem and love...'—there are those other than he who cannot understand her affections, and possibly don't even consider them as important: 'But to some others of more fine spirits, all these not seasoned with the presence of virtuous, discoursing and delightful friend have neither taste nor savour.'[33] This statement can be taken in two ways: either Burghley is speaking of the benefits of marriage and of a match formed out of love or mutual affection, or he is simply making a comment concerning other courtiers and councilors' inability to understand the personal benefits of this marriage to the queen.

He is also concerned that, by ruling alone, Elizabeth does not only have pressure on her in terms of the succession but also the incredibly exhausting task of governing a nation, which she did alone for over twenty years by this point. In this regard, he states: 'Who might command the whole world and had every necessary and every pleasure provided to her hand without pain or care, and no companion, friend or servant beloved on whom to bestow favours of that plenty...'[34] If the queen felt pressured by the growing opposition to her endeavour to marry Anjou, Burghley knew of it, and most likely received the brunt of her fury. His support for her would do no good. For so long, she had denied every opportunity given to her to marry a foreign prince so, if we are to go along with the accepted narrative that she was using Anjou for her own political means, then why is it so clearly evident that she was in love with him, far beyond the point of pretence? If she were at all unsure of her affections and serious intentions to finally marry a suitable prince for love as well as political gain, then why would so many of her subjects openly deny their support for this marriage, on paper and in song? Burghley's letter of support is equally evident in terms of her true affection for the duke. However, her feelings could not outweigh the voice of her people, and her duty to England.

What was Anjou's reaction to the overwhelming opposition to their marriage? It seems that in the months after Sidney and Stubbs's private and public expressions of disproval of the match, which likely resulted in a more one-sided public view of a marriage taking place, Anjou began to express his doubts of any nuptials occurring at all. In a letter dated 10th October 1579, the duke writes in his usual tone of fidelity and desire for Elizabeth but his impatience is also evident, with him stating that considering all things, he has resolved to betake himself to his own house, there to await 'her Majesty's command'. He further states that he hopes nostre singe [Simier] will bring him some favourable resolution but is much in doubt, having learnt from his last despatch that her Majesty had halted her parliament for a month in order to better understand 'the will of her people'. Following this, he adds that if Simier can bring him good news, he need not ask what reception he will meet with. He notes that 'there are many who envy him on that account but he need fear nothing so long as he has the happiness to enjoy her Majesty's good will'.[35]

A little over a month later, on 14th November, Anjou's frustrations had turned into desperation. He complained of being without any news from her and that it was: '…so unbearable that, if you don't please favour me with your readings, your Grenoulie [frog] cannot fere longer yve, and without the bandage which supports her there is some time he had died by his death proof of what he wanted most in his life…' He further complained of Simier's failings to help bring about a 'resolution'.[36]

So what exactly can we take from this letter? Certainly, Anjou is more than frustrated with the lack of an answer from Elizabeth and her council but his use of language serves a purpose. We cannot say for sure whether he wrote drafts of his letters to her, as she did, but his apparent pining for her favour, and use of her nickname for him – 'frog' – may have been his attempt to quicken her decision. Furthermore, his want for a 'resolution' in the matter is certainly evident but 'what he most wanted' can be interpreted in two different ways, and can certainly be dissected. Was what he most wanted Elizabeth, the woman and the queen, for his wife? Simply for herself and his love for her alone? Or, was what he most wanted a crown of his own with some measure of real power? This question may have crossed Elizabeth's mind at least once. She would soon have the opportunity to bask in the affections of her frog once more.

Elizabeth I coronation miniature by Nicholas Hilliard
c. 1600 after a lost original of c. 1559.

Young Elizabeth I portrait, attributed to William Scrots (c. 1546).

A portrait of Queen Katherine Parr (1512–1548), sixth and last wife of Henry VIII of England attributed to Master John (c.1600). Formerly thought to be Lady Jane Grey.

*Thomas Seymour, 1ˢᵗ Baron Seymour of Sudeley,
by Nicholas Denisot (c. 1547-1549).*

*William Cecil, Lord Burghley, Attributed to the Workshop
of Marcus Gheeraerts the Younger, c. 1580s.*

Robert Dudley, 1st Earl of Leicester, by an unknown artist (c. 1575).

*Lettice Knollys, Countess of Essex and Leicester,
attributed to George Gower (c.1585).*

*Prince Hercule-François, Duke of Alençon, later Duke of Anjou,
by an unknown artist, (c. 1572) .*

Catherine de' Medici and her children, by François Clouet, (1561).

Portrait of Elizabeth I of England Westminster school,
by an unknown artist (c.1580).

Chapter 6

Second Chances

Elizabeth and Anjou's marriage negotiations had caused more than a stir in England. Perhaps even more than her favouritism for Dudley. All of the queen's favourites were left waiting in the shadows until she tossed them a crumb of hope. Even Dudley, though not forgotten, was left reeling from her apparent love for Anjou. It would seem that her affections were genuine, considering she had risked her close relationship with Dudley and had the hands of her opponents cut off publically, not to mention Sir Philip Sidney's quick escape to the country. Along with Dudley's strong opposition, the Privy Council remained divided on the marriage. Meanwhile, Burghley's support and words of comfort in his letter to the queen did not seem to have the desired effect. It was most likely a relief to know that she had some form of support, yet she would not have been totally ignorant to the possible consequences of marrying Anjou, which many of her councillors warned of.

Still, the council would eventually agree that the queen had to make the final decision on the marriage herself. But was this what she really wanted? If she was delighted to hear that the ultimate decision was her own, she didn't show it. Though, by this point, she was desperate for an answer, she was also acutely aware of the undivided opposition to the marriage. However, it is likely that she hoped her council would eventually give way and unanimously accept the match. While the engagement was halted, it did not mean it was over. Her insistence that she be given two months to mull it over, and perhaps for her councillors to change their minds, was pragmatic. Though some historians have argued that this is where her affections seemed to unravel, it is more likely that this period gave her time to reflect on her feelings. Letters between the two of them continued, and talks upon the match would not have ceased entirely. Simier wrote multiple times to the queen, with reports and words of support and flattery. The duke himself would have been eager to keep the negotiations open, and so he continued to express his hopes that Elizabeth's council would grant their marriage.[1] As Simier had also left her court during the previous two months, it is clear the duke may have been worried that he would no longer have an ally on English soil, other than Lord Burghley. Simier's departure would have left the queen isolated from her duke, and risked the dilution of her affections. Thus, he also had any letters passed on from the duke, adorning them with pink seals and lovers' knots.[2] It is unsurprising that Elizabeth's affections did not grow stale over these months, as the letters from the duke and Simier were numerous.

By December of 1579, Anjou's patience was wearing thin, and though he continued to express his love and esteem for the queen, his tone seems somewhat severe. He states that he had hoped to receive an answer by this stage, and as it had been some time since they had seen one another, he hoped that any rumours about him and his actions had not changed her mind of him.[3] Elizabeth replied on 19th December. She addressed him as her 'dear' and discussed the political situation in Europe. Regarding their marriage, she wrote that she had been awaiting an answer from the commissioners, and stated:

> I am almost in agreement with the opinion of those who do not quit reminding you of my faults.

She also defends Simier, as by this stage Anjou had offended him in some manner. She pleads for her monkey:

> I ask some answer about Simier, for whom I wish some end to his unhappiness…

She then asks for the duke's forgiveness in the matter of the negotiations but states that she 'will not let my suit drop' and that 'my only request is that I always consider myself to be the same as I have been obliged to be dedicated to you…'.[4]

Many months passed, and in 1580, Anjou accepted the offer of sovereignty over the Netherlands by the State's General. This was a position once offered to Elizabeth, which she refused. Many historians have argued that this was her prime reason for re-opening the marriage negotiations that had fizzled out by early 1580.[5] However, other evidence suggests the opposite was the case. By the turn of 1581, negotiations would be once more in place. In April of that year, 'de Marchaumont',[6] the new French envoy, was chosen to invest a knighthood on the queen's behalf. The individual being knighted was Francis Drake. During the process of the task, Elizabeth dropped her garter and de Marchaumont requested that it be sent to Anjou. Though flattered, she exclaimed that she needed it to keep her stocking in place. However, it was sent to him later on. In the Elizabethan period, this was not such a shocking action for a woman, considering the cult of love and romance that had formed in the queen's court. However, Elizabeth was the monarch, and, thus, her courtiers would have taken this as an indication that the marriage was imminent.[7]

She had no option but to agree to a halt in the marriage negotiations until her council had further advice. Though they did encourage her to make her own decision, it seems that she was waiting, biding her time, and perhaps thinking upon the matter herself over a period of months. Her indecisive nature meant that she often took a long time to make a decision on a political matter but her marriage would probably have been the most important decision of her life, so it is not surprising that she took her time, keeping Anjou as close as possible through her letters. It seems that, during this time, their affection did not dwindle, and this would influence her later actions that would shock courtiers. She was approaching forty-seven, and it was confirmed that she was still capable of bearing a child. However, the reliability of any physician during this period must be questioned.[8]

Elizabeth knew that a match with Anjou really was her last chance at marriage. Her councillors' unanimous agreement that she should decide for herself would have left doubts in her mind as to her capability of making a successful marriage with the duke, despite their feelings for each other. Burghley noted that the queen shed 'many tears' on the matter of her hopes to marry Anjou and her council's inability to fully support her.[9] Her affections for the duke were clear to those in and around the court, as was her sadness towards the hostility to them. The Spanish Ambassador reported that the queen 'remained extremely sad' and that her irritation and melancholy was evident to those close to her. Her love letters continued, welcoming the return of the French commissioners assigned to come to a conclusion upon the finer details of the marriage negotiations. During the Elizabethan period, this would have been seen as a finalization of a marriage contract, and is indicative of Elizabeth's decision to continue forward with her plan to marry the man she loved.

She expressed her affections for Anjou and reconciled to marry him. He was later officially invited to return to her court, and this time, she was eager to make her subjects see that she was determined to keep her frog. When he returned, he possibly had hopes that he would remain there, or at least gain some security that it would become his home. When Elizabeth took the first move and sent Edward Stafford to France regarding political matters in the Netherlands and Anjou's sovereignty, it was most likely more important that he invite the duke to return to England to rekindle the marriage negotiations. To the queen's delight, although possibly not surprising, the duke was eager to give the match a second chance. Certainly, her letters hint that his feelings matched hers but could have been due to the pressure put on him by the king, or, more likely, his mother. Increasing pressure was put on French financial and military support due to the duke's claim to sovereignty in the Netherlands. This meant Catherine de Medici was even more reliant on her son's marriage to Elizabeth.[10]

It was important for her to keep Anjou's favour while he was *de facto* in exile following their first meeting and the council's unending negotiations. The commissioners for the marriage proposals were gathered. Elizabeth was, however, frustrated by them as much as she was dependent on them. Her letter written on 19th December 1579 indicates her frustration with them, stating: 'As for the commissioners, I believed that they will resemble words which, recited too many times, make the tongue slip out of order.'[11] This suggests that, though she was by this time exasperated with negotiations going nowhere, she was well aware of her tendency to lash out during times of great stress, though she is seemingly unapologetic in this matter. This letter was sealed and ready to be sent but was either not sent at all or recalled quickly, most likely due to her audience with Stafford upon his return, as she would have been informed of the members of the commission placed to see to her marriage plans. She was outraged by those chosen for the commission, given their lowly status. This prompted her to write another letter, and it is more likely this one was the dispatched version. Her displeasure is obvious, and her use of language strong:

I did not think before that France had been so ill furnished with princes and persons of good quality that they would be constrained to send me a child or man of low descent. I believe that they do it to diminish the greatness of my honour or to throw impediments in the way, so as not to send at all. I have, however, used roundness with regard to the king, sending to tell him by his ambassador that I would not allow a thing of so great importance to be disgraced because of hatred that may be borne to me.[12]

Prior to his arrival, the duke is said to have written to the queen of his desire for her, and to be 'kissing and rekissing all that your beautiful majesty can think of'. He added that he desired to be 'in bed between the sheets in your beautiful arms'.[13] Also, he stated in a letter that he hoped for a son, and that he referred to himself as the 'little Frenchman', and again as Elizabeth's 'slave'.[14] The language here is powerful. Not only does it indicate that the duke believed, or, rather, wished that the marriage would go ahead and that they would produce an heir, it also suggests that the queen would have most likely agreed with him and hoped for the same outcome. Otherwise, why would he use such strong sexual language, with implications of an heir to their union, if he did not believe that she was of the same inclination? It would seem too risky of a letter to send, considering the duke's future was now in the hands of the queen. Also, it is somewhat striking from the language in this letter that he became, in many ways, unashamedly subordinate to her, at least during this phase of their courtship. It cannot be denied that such letters would have caused scandal, and this is where Elizabeth's affections would have clouded her good judgement. If she was to have her way and marry Anjou, she could not allow for any scandal regarding their union. However, as was the case within the Tudor Court, rumours were to circulate surrounding the queen's virtue.

The argument that Elizabeth and Anjou had a sexual relationship upon his second visit to England seems unfounded. Though it is highly unlikely that they had sex, it does not mean their relationship wasn't sexual in terms of language, flirtations, and, even, in some context, touch. Elizabeth had many years of practice with Dudley in the art of lovemaking without actually having sex or touching at all. It was something she had to overcome in her youth. A female ruler's desires could not be fulfilled unless it was within the sanctity of matrimony. This is why it is doubtful that she slept with Anjou. The sexual tension between them is evident. But, if they wanted their courtship to be taken seriously, they would most likely have avoided too much intimacy in terms of physical touch. Certainly in company, and the queen was always in company. Still, rumours flourished. It was said that she visited the duke in his chamber during the day and night. Such rumours are actually written in letters and, therefore, it is evident that her court was busy with gossip. This was perhaps one of the most exciting times in over twenty years for the queen's courtiers, and they relished in it.

In a letter from Francis Anthony of Souza to Diego Botelho, who was in Antwerp at the time, he stated: 'There goes much babbling and the Queen doth not attend to other matters, but only to be together with the Duke in one Chamber from morning to noon, and afterwards till two or three hours after sunset. I cannot tell what a devil they do.'[15]

All too often, Anjou's last visit to England is either overlooked by historians, or deemed the point in which Elizabeth chose to rid herself of him once and for all. But the truth of the matter lies merged between these two interpretations. It was in November of 1581, when the duke returned to England for the second and last time in pursuit of Elizabeth's hand. He would not leave for some months. The queen seemed thoroughly excited by his stay, though some have construed this as her playing the part of an 'eager bride'. Towards later November, on a walk with the duke in the gallery, she openly kissed him and gave him a ring from her finger. Whether this is because a French diplomat happened to be approaching them or simply due to her own desire is uncertain, yet her words to the ambassador seem definitive and strong. She exclaimed: 'You write this to the King, that the Duke of Alençon shall be my husband.'[16]

It seems that the queen was doing her best to show her subjects that she was adamant to marry Anjou, despite their own afflictions. This may have been her only chance to convince those opposed to the duke's many virtues. Clearly, many would never see him in the same light as Elizabeth.

Her open displays of affection for him startled the gentlemen and ladies of her court, and no doubt the members of her council opposed to her marriage. Some have argued that due to the war in the Netherlands, the duke's invitation to England, and the queen's open affection at court were all a part of her ploy to keep him on her side at this crucial time. Yet, while this argument holds some merit in terms of the larger, more 'significant' events of the Wars of Religion, it ultimately overlooks any real possibility that she meant what she said.[17] The open hostility to her now-chosen suitor clearly had a detrimental effect on her state of mind and health overall. During the period of two months she was given prior to the duke's second visit, she complained of being unable to sleep, due to bad dreams.[18] It is, perhaps, this strain on her well-being and ability to function as sovereign that would lead to her eventually calling off the courtship.

She also complained to her physician that she had a 'severe pain in my throat continually this past fortnight'. Clearly, without Anjou and even Simier by her side, she had been a nervous wreck. But upon his return, she bloomed again. The duke's youth would have made her feel young and desired once more, though her longing for him in a more intimate way would have been repressed.[19] An interesting take on her own feelings about her councilors' general opposition to her choice in Anjou, is that she actually felt too insecure in her own reign to go above the men who advised her. This seems likely. Reports state that she often exploded into a rage and railed against her council because of their inability to take her side on the matter. But did she really need to take their advice? They had, in fact, left the decision in her hands. Yet, it is most likely that this was a tactic on her council's part due to their knowledge of her insecurity and indecisive nature.[20]

According to Elizabeth, 'they all', meaning her Privy Council, had their own families and other measures of support to love them, and she had nobody. Though not all of her council members had families, and she was constantly surrounded by friends and family members, it is most likely that she was speaking from a maternal point of view. She was now approaching old age, and it is likely that she was experiencing menopause, which would explain her frequent outbursts of rage, many tears, bad dreams, and general bouts of feeling unwell and melancholic. For years, her council pushed many foreign suitors under her nose because they suited the council's agenda but this would have left her even more insecure over the succession and her father's line, and it is certain that she would have wanted to carry out his wishes to continue the dynasty. Although, there are some who have argued the complete opposite. In many ways, Elizabeth's insecurities are apparent in her letters to Anjou. If she didn't marry when she had one last chance because she had little support from her council, it would suggest that she was far less capable of expressing her own personal power in terms of foreign policy, unlike her father, and even her sister, who evidently did not accept their councilors' advice regarding who they chose to marry. To them, marriage was of a personal matter to the monarch, and once it produced an heir, it had little to do with their subjects. However, as Elizabeth heeded the advice of her council, it is evident that it did have everything to do with them.[21]

The queen had more supporters than just Burghley. Many flocked to back her endeavour to marry Anjou, mostly due to their belief that the French match was of political necessity. For the new year of 1580, she was given a gift of *Partheniads* by George Puttenham, who wrote one of the earliest recorded treatises on poetry as an art form rather than a craft. The name *Partheniads* in itself is suggestive in an informal way of Homer's *Iliad*. Though certainly playful, at least two poems from this series are suggestive of Puttenham's support for Elizabeth's marriage to Anjou. Though it has been mentioned by some historians that his poetry suggests his support for the match, such literature has not been considered in determining the true nature behind their courtship. Surely, by this time, it was well known amongst courtiers that the queen was in love with the duke. She made no secret of the fact.[22] In one poem, Puttenham depicts her as a glorious flower, whose beauty would remain but only for a time, and one-day fade. In the same verse, the poem also laments her lack of a child and heir, which he deems undesirable to her people:

'Woe and Alas' the people cry and shriek,
Why fades this flower and leaves no fruit nor seed?[23]

This is indicative of the sadness and chaos looming over England due to her lack of an heir. Who would she leave behind her to secure England's safety and prosperity? Another one of Puttenham's poems likens Elizabeth to a ship, alluding to the lily, which in French is *Fleur de lis.* This is suggestive, yet the language is subtle enough. The lily in question is symbolic and emblematic of the French crown. Therefore, Elizabeth is the ship, but 'None but a king or more may her aboard'.[24]

She was not ignorant of the support for her marriage to Anjou, yet, without the unanimous agreement of her council, she found it difficult to come to a decision by herself. Even so, it does seem that, by November of 1581, she was sure of her love for the duke, and her intentions to marry him. Unusually for Elizabeth, though she displayed her authority as England's queen in a rather 'kingly' fashion, often outwardly going against the expectations of women for the day, she was also careful to seemingly place herself beneath Anjou in terms of their relationship dynamic. It seems she was keen to play the part of the dutiful wife, subordinate to her husband, even prior to any agreement that they would marry. This is evident as far back as their first correspondence prior to the duke's initial visit in 1579, where she stated in a letter regarding his wish to visit her:

I recognize my lack of wit to instruct you, you may accept it as from one who will never have a thought not dedicated to your honour and will never betray you by her advice, but will give it as if my soul depended thereon.[25]

It seems somewhat confusing that she was able to submit herself to Anjou's will in her letters, yet found it difficult to accept him as her better in terms of personal power. She was, in every sense, a paradox. It was acceptable that she would display her supposed natural weakness in her femininity as a wife but not as a sovereign. In many ways, it seems it was a way of letting Anjou know that he held some power in the relationship. If she wanted to keep him, she would need to be careful not to belittle his masculinity.

While her outburst in front of the French diplomat during Anjou's second stay at the English court may have worked in securing the duke's commitment to the match, she was also aware that what she wanted and what her people would allow were two entirely different things. Burghley felt that her openness in front of the French diplomat about her intention to marry Anjou was clever and he praised her for it. When the duke arrived in England, Elizabeth wrote to Burghley: 'Let me know what you wish me to do'.[26] It would seem that, though she had Burghley's support, if the time came for her to take his advice, whatever it may be, she was prepared to take it for the sake of her country. In this, we can see that in the end, her sense of duty came before her affections for Anjou. She was able to separate her duty as a monarch and her role in her courtship with the duke in terms of her language, actions, and intentions. Yet, this could only last for a time and she was obviously aware of this. In the end, she knew that if she could not gain the support of her people and their trust in Anjou, then she would have to submit, regardless of her feelings for him.

So, what was Anjou's reaction to her sense of duty? How did

he feel about her placing her country over him, yet outwardly stating her undying love and intention to marry him? Certainly, he found her perplexing. When she informed him that, in terms of religion, her people would not allow for her consort to worship the Roman Catholic religion, openly or privately, she stated that, if he was insistent on doing so, then she would have to consider the advice of her council and call off any marriage negotiations.[27] This frustrated the duke, yet it shows Elizabeth's ability to think rationally about her future. There was little he could do or say on this matter. The depiction of him dangling at her will seems not so far from reality. Though she may have loved him, she loved her people more, and certainly valued her position as queen more than any man. Anjou, having put so much effort into this courtship, felt that her council had exhausted the point of religion. It seems that he was ever hopeful that she would eventually go over her council's advice and marry him, anyway. He was to be greatly disappointed.[28]

The commission's presence in England prior to the duke's second visit brought mounting tensions to a head. Hardheaded Protestants were disgusted by the expensive spectacles and large banquets in honour of Anjou and the French party, with the Massacre of St. Bartholomew's Eve still in their minds. Mendoza reported that Dudley and many other nobles were prepared to gather their kinsmen and other followers if the necessity for protection against any Catholic coup were to arise. The money Elizabeth spent in preparation for the commission, and later during the duke's second and final stay in England, says a lot about her true feelings for him, considering she was always so frugal in terms of her spending. By the time she came to the throne after her sister's death, England was not the wealthy kingdom it had been during her grandfather and father's reigns. She had to be careful, and her wardrobe was often recycled. In essence, she was a queen on a budget. So, when she spent a fortune for a new banqueting hall to be erected for the commissioner's stay, her people were astounded.

On St. George's Day, 23rd April 1581, she threw a huge banquet. Her excessiveness in dress and splendour, along with diamonds and rare stones galore, the mass of paintings, and endless trays of sweetmeats, were perhaps a waste of English money on a cause that would never prevail. This shows that the queen was still serious by the time her final attempts to marry Anjou came about. The expense to the royal coffers would have been too much otherwise.[29] By the time the duke arrived in England in 1581, she became aware that Catherine de Medici was yet again speaking to the Spanish in terms of a match with a bride for her son should his efforts in England fail. It is clear that Catherine was as shrewd as queen regents came, and she made it her business to seek profitable marriage for all her children.

Yet, Anjou's desire for Elizabeth was by this point evident. If his letters in pursuit of the queen's bed did not make this clear, then her own tendency to lavish him with gifts and attention certainly did. He would have felt every bit the king-in-waiting. With the queen and her frog prince seemingly intent on marrying, and this time with his stay not being a secret, the court was becoming used to his presence.[30] Yet, something was amiss. Dudley was seemingly supportive of the match, even openly courteous to Anjou, and if he was jealous of Elizabeth's intimacy with the duke, he didn't show it. He publicly announced that their marriage was the only way to 'secure the tranquility of England'. Ross has suggested that the only reason for his apparent complacently was because he knew the marriage would never actually come about.[31] This seems valid, and it may have been the case that everyone besides Elizabeth and Anjou was aware that their union would never become official.

Interestingly, Walsingham was also showing signs of being well disposed to, if not supporting, the match, at least outwardly. This was strange behaviour considering he had once been so fervently opposed to it. Elizabeth's dramatic performance in front of the French Ambassador at the beginning of Anjou's stay in England cooled any discontentment that the duke felt regarding the long wait for an answer as to whether he would be her husband. Ever the pragmatist, she would have had many reasons for this public show of affection. Besides trying to convince her courtiers and council that their intentions to marry were genuine and borne of true affection, she would have also felt the pressure to keep him interested. After all, she had kept him waiting for an answer longer than any other suitor. The duke was touched by her gesture in giving him a ring, and it is said that he gave her one in return, from his own finger.[32] This event was not only crucial in terms of understanding the true affection between them but it also allows for an insight into their views of how the matter was going to turn out. Was this their only chance to exchange rings? Certainly, it was the only time the pair would do so. In a way, it may have been Elizabeth's way of finalizing their courtship. Perhaps it was even a sign of her expressing what she so deeply wanted but knew she could not have. Anjou's attendants and followers would have been overjoyed by these small gestures.

He apparently had other motivations for his return to England: Money. This was to help fund his endeavours in the Netherlands. It has been suggested by some that this was the only reason he waited on Elizabeth's answer for so long. In hindsight, it is obvious that he needed the queen much more than she needed him, and this may have influenced her final decision to end the courtship. Between October 1581 and February 1582, her esteem for the duke seems to have diminished in many ways. Whether that was due to his actions or the stance of her council and subjects is debatable. That doesn't mean she did not still hold affection for him. On the contrary, her later writings suggest she may well have regretted her decision.

Her final decision would not come from the influences of Burghley – her 'spirit', nor Walsingham – her 'moor', or even

Dudley – her 'eyes'. It came from herself. In the end, her head had to rule over her heart. This doesn't mean she liked or loved Anjou any less. She most likely loved him more than he loved her – and her apparent wealth. However, the queen loved her country, subjects, and herself more. Though the duke would deny the genuine nature behind the reasons for her final decision – religion – the reality was that the risk of a marriage to a foreign and Catholic prince was too great. There were already enemies within the kingdom – even within the court – that saw Elizabeth as a usurper, sitting in place of the true queen, Mary, Queen of Scots. At this point, Mary was under house arrest in Sheffield, and the number of followers for her cause was ever-growing. This threatened the Protestant hold over England and, thus, with Catholics surrounding the country at every angle, the marriage to Anjou would be the final nail in the coffin for Elizabeth's Protestant kingdom. She could never have married the duke without great consequence. Even during his second visit in 1581, her ministers were under threat from a Catholic conspiracy from within.[33]

As Catholic rebels were being repressed, even by December of 1580 during Anjou's stay, it became harder and harder for Elizabeth to maintain her argument for her marriage to him. She was soon to witness the consequences of the Catholic threat in the actions of her parliament. By 1581, an act would be passed to 'retain the queen's majesty's subjects in their due obedience'. This prohibited any subject, noble or not, from conforming to the Roman Catholic cause and converting. The hearing of Mass was to be severely punished. If she had married Anjou, these later actions may have never come about, or at least caused a rift in their union. Thus, the outcome of this courtship probably could never have been altered. If she did choose to marry the duke out of love rather than reason, she may have paid well in consequence. The more the Catholic rebellion pushed against her administration, the less she liked the idea of the marriage. Though she was frustrated with Walsingham and other members of her council, they were equally as exasperated by her affections for Anjou.[34]

Yet, Walsingham was not like Burghley. He did not know his queen as well as her 'spirit'. Elizabeth was clearly insecure in her reign in a number of ways, with marriage, or lack of it, thereof, being one of these insecurities. Walsingham did not see this and often referred to Elizabeth in her presence as 'in a deep sleep and heedlessly secure'.[35] As Helen Castor perfectly put it, Walsingham 'could not see that his insomniac queen, whose life had never been safe, had developed a different understanding of where the route to personal and political security might lie.'[36] Elizabeth had probably never felt safe in her reign, and therefore it is clear why she remained so indecisive for most of her life. This would have had a much larger impact in terms of the Catholic coup surrounding her. If she married Anjou, she was doomed. It is also likely that she worried about factors other than religion. The idea of sex, or any real intimacy at all, may have startled the queen, who, if it is to be believed, was a virgin and forty-eight by the end of the duke's second visit. Her traumatic childhood and adolescence at the hands of her father and then her stepfather may have influenced her eventual refusal of Anjou. Though she may have enjoyed the idea of sex and had a genuine lust for him, the reality of it and its consequences – pregnancy and childbirth – most likely terrified her. Though, again, it is highly unlikely that she was able to produce an heir at this point, despite her physician's beliefs.

For a time, she kept up her duties as a hostess and, in terms of the courtship, paid homage to Anjou, threw more banquets, and lavished him with gifts. Yet, her reported health at the time is indicative of her true sentiments by the end of this courtship. She was afraid. It is known that she was kept up at night with headaches, a possible consequence of being forced to hide her true feelings for some time so as not to offend

Anjou and the French in general. The threat of a Catholic coup could not diminish love entirely, though. The fact that she tried hard to cover her true worries and keep the duke happy for a time could indicate her true feelings for him. Some historians, though, believe that by this time, any affection she may have had for him was gone, and that she simply wished to keep the possibility of an alliance open. Even the Spanish Ambassador reported that he was unconvinced by her overt displays of affection for Anjou in public.[37]

Interestingly, Elizabeth's women, or ladies of the bedchamber and maids of honour, were also to put pressure on her in their opposition to the match, for the sake of her health. It is their reports of an increase in her insomnia that show the real consequences of her loving a man she could not have. She was reportedly afraid of the dark, something Guy has mentioned on more than one occasion.[38] The stress and sadness she felt, knowing she would have to eventually let the duke down for a third time, would have had a profound effect on this already existing disorder. It was reported that, during his second stay, she insisted that one or more of her ladies sleep beside her on a palette bed to comfort her, which was also a common practice for the period. But her ladies were also seemingly responsible for her change in mood. Guy mentions that they 'wept and wailed' when she stated that she was serious about marrying Anjou, and, believing their queen, they vexed and terrified her into a dark state of mind that she could not return from. Her inability to sleep, which worsened during this time, and reports of her dulling mood, are indicative of this factor. She is said to have spent the nights of Anjou's visit 'in doubts and cares without sleep'.[39]

The fact that her ladies had some influence on her final decision about her marriage to the duke is telling in more than one way. Firstly, it shows her closeness to the many women who served her and her dependency on their approval. It is also a good indication of how most of her courtiers felt about her match to Anjou. She depended on her ladies for most daily tasks, like getting dressed. Therefore, their council would have been heeded on more than one occasion. Secondly, it seems that her ladies really did believe that their queen would marry the duke, and their reactions to this is a sign of her true feelings for him. If she was in any way hesitant about these feelings, her ladies would have known. She spent most of her time in the company of these women and, therefore, it can be suggested that they knew her more than anyone else. Her ladies did not doubt that their queen loved her frog truly.

The great opposition against the match, along with the Catholic threat, and Elizabeth's inability to sleep well or think clearly, not only meant that she could no longer enjoy her courtship but also that she would never again feel safe or confident in her reign if she married him. Therefore, her final decision is understandable. After many weeks of melancholy, bad dreams mixed with insomnia, and perhaps many tears, she decided to end her courtship with her frog prince and put the idea of marriage away for good. It was probably for the best in terms of her health and security, yet it would have been a real blow for her as well as the duke. She had failed in some of her most important duties as queen: marrying, possibly producing a male heir to the Tudor dynasty, and ensuring England's safety. However, the story of this incredible courtship does not end here. Elizabeth and Anjou would remain connected for the rest of his short life. Though their marriage was an impossible endeavour, their love, to whatever capacity, seems to have been true and real, at least from Elizabeth's point of view. This affection would continue.

Chapter 7

The Question of Succession

During Elizabeth's long reign, the question of who would succeed her was always at the forefront of her council's objectives. When she came to the throne in 1558 at the age of twenty-five, she was still considered relatively young. She was also reported to have been quite the beauty. Whether this was true or simply an interpretation of courtly flattery towards the monarch is uncertain. If her portraits from the time can be trusted, the reports would seem to be accurate, albeit the lack of pock marks. So, it would have seemed something of an easy task for her councillors to guide her to choose a suitable foreign prince or noble to marry and thus produce an heir to continue her father's line. However, those who did not already know of Elizabeth's opposition to marriage in her early years as queen, would be sorely disappointed. Though her ascension was marked by controversy due to her gender, much like her sister Mary's, Elizabeth was different, and had no intention of being the dutiful wife, subdued and humble. Mary I may have been the perfect example of what a queen should be, or, rather, a queen-consort, but the monarch Elizabeth would become was far from what others expected.

We already know that she was careful to play the part of a 'meek and feeble woman', but it is also apparent that she flaunted her femininity when necessary, making no hint of remorse in regards to her gender earlier on in her reign. It may have been the case that the young queen was simply content to be alive after the trauma of the past few years, happy to finally be called by God to rule England. She was aware that her council wished her to marry and produce an heir, and they would have vented their frustrations for her to choose a suitable husband. For the men who surrounded her throughout her reign, they could not understand why their queen did not wish to marry and produce an heir for the safety of the realm.[1] Marriage, in Elizabethan England, was typically followed by a child. Not always, but it was generally accepted that a wife would produce an heir for her husband's name, and, if she were a queen, an heir for her kingdom.

Often, Tudor brides became pregnant quickly, and if they didn't, they were considered 'barren'. Also, the trauma of childbirth could have devastating effects. Women did not always survive the severity of childbirth in an age where little was known about the body and female anatomy, never mind the process of childbirth and the threat of infection and other factors. The essential purpose of a woman was to become a wife and to produce children, and Elizabeth was no exception. It would have been considered her first and primal duty as the new sovereign to marry and produce a male heir.[2] So, the questions have since remained: why did Elizabeth not marry when she could? Did she not want to give England an heir to the Tudor dynasty? Was she barren? Was she more afraid of childbirth or being subdued by a man? If she did not marry and have a child, who did that leave as her successor?

Though the new queen's ascension was widely celebrated in England, the rest of Europe had a different view. She was 'illegitimate', a 'usurper', and a 'heretic'. Most likely, her rise to the throne was more irritating to others because she was a Protestant, a woman, and a stark reminder of her father's dismissal of the Catholic Katherine of Aragon in favour of Elizabeth's mother Anne Boleyn – a reformer. The rest of Europe felt that her cousin, Mary, Queen of Scots, was the true Catholic heir to England. This implies that the problem with Elizabeth was more about religion than her gender. Her sister was a queen, and so was her cousin – the two Mary's seen as everything 'a queen' should be. But Elizabeth wasn't about to become what was understood to be a queen. In every sense, she would become a female king. That is until she met the Duke of Anjou, much later in her reign, when the threat of Catholic Europe was greatest, and the possibility of her producing an heir for England was at its lowest. In the context of being expected to produce a legitimate heir, it is only now considered, through hindsight, that she gave England something much better.

The men surrounding her – appointed to advise her – may well have been desperate for her to reproduce, and there was no reason to think she was incapable of the task. Yet, they were also acutely aware that in order for her marriage to produce an heir, the queen had to be physically and sexually attracted to her chosen husband. During the Tudor period – and this theory possibly goes far back into the medieval period – it was believed there was some connection between conception and female pleasure during intercourse. If a woman was to enjoy a healthy sex life with a relatively handsome and pleasing spouse, then there was little doubt she would produce a healthy brood of children. The current representation of Elizabeth as 'The Virgin Queen' and 'Gloriana', who became the celebration of purity due to her opposition to marriage and of any form of eroticism, was created towards the end of her life and mostly after her death. Therefore, the idea of her remaining a virgin without giving her kingdom an heir was not even a consideration.[3] Interestingly, this perception of the queen has been challenged due to new considerations regarding her political stance, her psychological state due to the trauma of probable molestation in her teenage years, and her later courtship with her 'frog', the Duke of Anjou. The iconic symbol of Elizabeth as the virgin may have warmed the hearts of Englishmen later on in her reign and after her death in 1603, but this was far from the case during the early and middle periods when her council's only prerogative was that she should be warming the marital bed.

In terms of taking on a husband in her early reign, John

Knox stated that, as a woman, a female ruler should be subject to the will of men, and, therefore, a husband. This suggests that Knox felt a woman ruling alone without male governance was unnatural. If Elizabeth was to go with what Knox had stated in *The First Blast of the Trumpet Against the Monstrous Regiment of Women,* from 1558, her marriage and production of a male heir was the will of God: 'But now to the second part of nature, in the which I include the revealed will and perfect ordinance of God, and against this part of nature, I say, that it doth manifestly repugne that any woman shall reign or bear dominion over man.'[4]

However, Knox's views against a female power are unlikely to have caused her any strain, especially so early in her reign. Her sister Mary had exiled him, and it is more likely that his writings were intended for Mary of Guise and Mary, Queen of Scots, who would both rule his homeland of Scotland. It seems that, though Elizabeth may have worried about her own personal power being compromised by marrying, she needn't have. Many historians today argue that she was unwilling to marry as she did not wish to share power. Though this argument is true, it doesn't seem to be the sole reason why she never married. It is clear from her courtship with Anjou during her mid-reign that she was willing to marry, and well able to state her conditions in terms of personal power and who wielded it. The true reason for her reluctance to marry goes deeper and is much more psychological than that of vanity and power. She had support in terms of ruling alone as a woman, and though many wanted her to produce a healthy son to succeed her, many were also ready to support her as a lone female ruler. For example, in 1559, John Aylmer argued that though Knox was correct in stating that a woman was answerable to her husband in all matters, as a queen, Elizabeth was first and foremost primarily answerable to God. Knox was also careful himself to note upon Elizabeth's succession that she was an 'exceptional monarch'.[5]

So, if she was initially secure enough in the support for her position as queen, was she secure in the knowledge that her council would not repossess that support if she did not produce an heir? It seems, for all the love of her court, council, and subjects, Elizabeth alone, without a spouse and an heir, was not satisfactory enough. Though she did rule alone and died without providing an heir, it is clear that her decision to never marry – even Anjou, despite her obvious affection for him – caused more problems for her than it solved. If she was never to marry, who would succeed her? The answer to that question added perhaps more strain to the Protestant Elizabeth and to her council. Religious issues had always dominated the early years of her reign but, by the time she had been on the throne for twenty-odd years, and about to embark on her courtship with Anjou, the question was not simply of who she would marry but when she would marry. Her first speech before her parliament in 1559 would have echoed down through the decades of her reign and, quite like her namesake Elizabeth II, her declaration before her subjects was something she lived by. In her first speech, she stated she was not opposed to marrying, if God should find it suitable for her to take a husband, but if he found it agreeable that she should rule alone, she would obey him.[6] But if Elizabeth was governor of the Church of England – God's representative in England – then wasn't her will his command? This was a clever tactic to get out of her obligation to marry. However, she would be hounded for most of her reign to take on a husband, until, ironically, when she found one suitable in Anjou, she was begged to remain alone in her position.

Prior to her ascension, she had many suitors in pursuit of the hand of a princess. This included the Duke of Savoy. Yet, from the start, it was clear she had no intention of producing an heir to the throne, because she was so insistent on remaining unmarried. The alternative to Elizabeth's position was frightening to her council, and a threat to the establishment of the Protestant religion's dominance. 1567 was a rough year for the queen in terms of the pressure put on her regarding the succession. If she was adamant not to marry, then she should name an heir. But everyone knew who that heir had to be, and nobody was willing to accept her terms. Burghley mentioned to the queen that if she did not marry and produce an heir, then her subjects would find this unsettling. The fact that she should even consider choosing her own heir was also deeply worrying. Yet, Burghley need not have worried, Elizabeth was never going to name an heir to her throne when she was fit and healthy and well able to rule on her own terms. It was Mary Stuart who became the thorn in her side. Queen of Scotland since 1542, she returned there after the death of her husband, Francis II, King of France, in 1561.

Though Scotland was a Protestant country by the time Mary returned to her homeland – her brother was ruling in her name – she was a Catholic. This made her not only a danger to the established Protestant church in Scotland but also a threat to the Tudor dynasty in England, because Elizabeth was unmarried and without an heir. By 1567, Mary had married for a second time, to Lord Darnley, a cousin to both her and Elizabeth. He was also an English subject. Elizabeth, Mary, and Darnley were all descended from Henry VII – Elizabeth through Henry VIII, and Mary and Darnley through Princess Margaret Tudor of England, Henry VIII's sister.[7] Mary and Darnley both had a good claim to Elizabeth's throne, and without an heir of her own, Mary's son, James Stuart, also had a claim to the throne of England. While Mary was always a threat to Elizabeth, the two queens often wrote to one another. Yet, when she claimed to be Elizabeth's sole heir, even *de facto* true queen of England, Elizabeth was furious. But she was not to worry – by 1568, Lord Darnley was dead, a suspected murder, by order of none other than Mary, Queen of Scots.

This scandal had a dire effect on Mary's position and power, and though Elizabeth would have been in a better position due to the controversy, she supported her cousin, but would refuse to openly show this support or to ever name her as her heir. In 1568, she wrote to Mary regarding Darnley's death: 'My ears have been so deafened and my understanding so grieved and my heart so affrighted to hear the dreadful news of the abominable murder of your husband and my killed cousin...'[8]

Mary would ultimately lose her throne and her homeland, yet she didn't have to travel far to find support for her claim to another – Elizabeth's.[9] It may seem unlikely but her claim to the English throne would have a detrimental effect on Elizabeth's view towards marriage and childbearing, and although Mary was imprisoned by the time Elizabeth started courting Anjou, between 1578 and 1582, her claim to the throne was never far from the queen's mind. This would have a profound effect on Elizabeth's later decision to end her courtship with Anjou, and any possibility of her producing an heir to the Tudor dynasty.

The rumours of Mary's involvement in her second husband's death caused Elizabeth to establish a commission of inquiry. This was conducted mostly from Westminster, where she could keep an eye on proceedings. Secret talks were already in motion about marrying Mary to another English noble, the Duke of Norfolk, though Elizabeth was seemingly unaware of this. Mary, too, had taken things into her own hands and married a Scottish noble, the Earl of Bothwell. Most know this story well. She was eventually forced to abdicate, fled to England for Elizabeth's help, only to be imprisoned in a small remote castle. Elizabeth could not openly support Mary's cause, nor declare her as her heir due to the scandal she had caused, along with the fact that she was a Catholic, but she had helped defuse tensions within Scotland and between both kingdoms, which shared the same island. Mary's son James, at this point a child king, and later Elizabeth's successor, was taken into the ward of his uncle, the Earl of Moray, who acted as his regent. Surely Elizabeth's reign was secure now, with any threat from Mary Stuart put down?

However, this was far from the case, with the queen still needing a legitimate heir of her own.[10]

Many appealed to her to openly take on Mary as her heir, and to treat her for what she was, a fellow queen and family member. But she was hesitant. All she had worked for in terms of securing the establishment of the Protestant religion once again in England was at stake because of one simple flaw within Mary: her Catholicism. It was apparent to her that Mary had many flaws, which led to her abdication in Scotland, though many historians argue this point on how involved Mary was in her own downfall. She laid claim to Elizabeth's throne from as early as 1558 – her coat of arms, depicting lions, symbolized her claim to the English crown. The Bishop of Ross, John Lesley, was amongst the few who petitioned Elizabeth in terms of taking Mary on as her official heir, even recognizing her as a daughter. Perhaps, in hindsight of the outcome of the queen's final courtship with Anjou, this may well have been an easier decision.[11]

She found no rational reason to announce Mary as her successor. Mary was a Catholic, frivolous, impulsive, and had shown herself to be incapable of ruling on her own. Yet, for all her flaws, she did carry out her most important duty – she gave Scotland a prince, a future king. Elizabeth had not done this for England. There was no question by this point that she could produce an heir at all. Again, her physicians stated that she was capable and her council still had time to find her a suitable match. However, there were rumours at home and abroad that the queen was barren, and, thus, could never carry out the great duty that the now-disgraced queen of Scots had. Was she actually capable of conceiving a child? And were Anjou's hopes of a male heir from her founded on false hopes? Could the Virgin Queen actually carry out this important duty, if she wanted to?

Whether Elizabeth really was the 'Virgin Queen' or not has been hotly debated for centuries. Even during her own lifetime, she was subject to rumours that she had a sexual relationship with Dudley and, later on in her life, when she should have been free of such implications, they were brought up again, only this time they involved her frog prince. Another debate regarding her private life is whether she was fertile or not. Some have debated that she was capable of conceiving and others have promoted a number of medical reasons that would have restricted her ability to bear a child. The truth is, we will never know for sure. Medical training and knowledge of the reproductive system and how it actually functioned was limited during the sixteenth and seventeenth centuries. For many decades after Elizabeth's death, little changed in regards to how conception and childbirth were viewed publically and professionally. It will never be known for sure whether she had entered into a full-blown sexual relationship with Dudley in her youth. As mentioned before, she probably would not have risked intercourse, considering her position and her traumatic past.[12] It is also most likely that she did not enter into a sexual relationship with Anjou in the 1580s. This would have been pointless during the negotiations, or even when the duke stayed in England, as they probably believed they would eventually marry, anyway. Little did they know what lay ahead.

With the question that Elizabeth would have considered engaging in intercourse either as a young or ageing woman put aside, was she really able to become pregnant in the first place? By the time she was courting Anjou and awaiting an answer from her council regarding their marriage, he was still in his twenties and she in her late forties. The question of the queen's fertility was an important issue. It was obvious to many, not least her own ladies, that she was incapable of conceiving a child at this point. It is likely, due to the state of her health, that she was already in the midst of menopause. Many felt that her courtship was pointless due to her clear inability to produce an heir. There exists a tract within the Venetian State Papers that states: 'It is impossible to hope for posterity from a woman of the Queen's age, and of so poor and shattered a constitution as hers.'[13]

Burghley, as we know, was by this stage generally in favour of the French match, or of any match at all. He took the matter into his own hands and had Elizabeth examined by some of the best physicians, concluding that the queen was well capable of producing children. Though it may have been unusual for her age, especially for the time, it was not impossible that she was capable of conceiving. Burghley even questioned her ladies in terms of her menstrual cycle. Certainly, by the time she was courting the duke, she was fond of the idea of giving England an heir, and it is evident from their letters that they really hoped it was possible. Dudley, for one, was of the opinion that it would be unsafe for her to even contemplate having a child at this point, due to her age and the dangers of childbirth. Though childbirth was a much more dangerous task during the Tudor period than it is today, it is more likely that his opposition to the idea was down to his dislike of Anjou and his opposition to the French match. Whether his hostility was due to personal or political reasons is down to speculation but the answer probably lies somewhere in between. Elizabeth took no heed of his warning of Anjou or the perils of childbirth, considering his latest scandal in marrying Lettice Knollys.

Some historians and authors have speculated on whether Elizabeth actually had an illegitimate child. Rumours were circulating that she had more than one, and for more than one man. If this were true, then her fertility during her youth, at least, could be confirmed. It would also allow for an insight into why she opposed marriage in her youth, and why she only thought to renegotiate the idea later on in her life when she met Anjou. The reality is unclear. Certainly, these rumours circulated in the court throughout her later reign and trickled down through history into the public imagination through popular works and adaptations. But were these just rumours? And what did this matter in relation to her courtship with Anjou? One rumour was that she had a child with Thomas Seymour, her stepmother's new husband, and as early as 1548. This would have made her fifteen years old giving birth, possibly sixteen. Could a Tudor princess, whether legitimized or not by this point, really get away with having a secret love child? It happened before, but that would mean either Elizabeth entered into a sexual relationship with her stepfather, or she was raped. This only adds further fuel to the belief that Seymour was molesting her for some time.[14]

There is the theory that she felt some affection for Seymour. If this is the case, a possible secret birth and his subsequent execution would have been enough to put the young queen off marriage in the early years of her reign. Her intimate relationship with him, whether consensual or not, may have affected her psychologically, and so had an effect on her later opposition to marriage and childbirth. This has been challenged, with many historians stating that we cannot interpret Elizabeth's experience by modern standards of psychological analysis and modern conceptions of what is consensual and what is not. This may be but the fact is, Elizabeth's mental state could well have been affected, not just by the context of her relationship with Seymour but by the trauma of any possible childbirth. Though, because this theory is simply based on rumour, it can be determined that any possible trauma inflicted upon her was due to the rumours themselves, and the consequences they would have for her reputation and future reign.

Due to her alleged sexual liaison with Seymour, her stepmother sent her away from their home in May of 1548. Jones has questioned whether this was to punish her, or to save her and protect her from Thomas. Katherine herself was pregnant by this time. If Elizabeth became pregnant, she would have had to confide in her stepmother. Thus, her time away for some months could be seen as a secret confinement in wait of the birth. Conveniently, she could have given birth sometime around

October, which would have coincided with the aftermath of Katherine's death in September. Jones's argument seems to hold some merit, and the dates fit. However, her use of sources in regards to this argument seem somewhat biased. The contents of Elizabeth's letter to the Lord Protector in January of 1549, reading the 'shameful slanders' that she was pregnant have been interpreted here to suit a particular narrative. Such a secret would be hard to keep, and Elizabeth was surrounded by attendants and servants wherever she lived and wherever she went. If there was any truth to the rumours, somebody had betrayed her.[15]

However, in June of 1548, an even earlier letter which Elizabeth wrote to her stepmother from Cheston, during this period of disgrace, indicates a very different reason for her being sent away. She had to be careful and her letter shows her understanding of the need to safeguard her reputation. This may well have been the beginnings of her resolve to never marry. Here, she wrote:

Although I coulde not be plentiful in giving thankes for the manifold kindenis received at your hithnis hande at my departure, yet I am some thinge to be borne with al, for truly I was replete with sorowe to departe frome your highnnis, especially leaving you undoubtful of helthe, and albeit I answered litel I wayed it more dipper when you sayd you wolde warne me of al evelles that you shulde hire of me...'

She continues: '...but what may I more say than thanke God for providinge suche frendes to me, desiringe God to enriche me with ther longe life, and me grace to be in hart no les thankeful to receyve it, than I nowe am glad in writinge to shewe it.'[16]

This not only indicates Elizabeth's love for her stepmother but could also suggest that she was grateful for Katherine's decision to have her sent as far away from Seymour as possible. It could also indicate a hint of Elizabeth's remorse for the events that took place, but this is not clear. There is no hint of a hidden pregnancy in this letter and it seems that Katherine's decision to send her away was simply to save the reputations of all involved.

It has been speculated that, even throughout her reign, Elizabeth gave birth to many children and often went on progress as a means of hiding them. Though this makes sense, there is no hard evidence to suggest that keeping many pregnancies a secret from the public was possible. It has been suggested that she had at least one son for Dudley, and though these rumours would have an effect on her later during her reign, they did not seem to deter Anjou's intention to marry her. Nor did the rumours of past pregnancies deter her from wanting to have a child with him. If she did have at least one illegitimate child, it could explain Burghley's confidence that she was capable of having a healthy child, and, therefore, his support for her proposed marriage to the duke. This is all speculation, of course, but even so, the rumours have been passed down through history and remain active in popular imagination. Some interpretations of Elizabeth's image as the iconic, pure, chaste, 'Virgin Queen' are thought to have originated from Tudor propaganda used to hide the fact that she actually was none of the above.

For the most part, it is believed that she was a virgin and, without any hard evidence to suggest otherwise, it is unlikely that she give birth to any illegitimate children or even entered into a sexual relationship. Though, by the time she was approaching fifty, she was adamant that she would marry Anjou and produce an heir. It could be suggested that her insistence that a marriage to Anjou could produce an heir was a sign of her true affection for him, especially since she had never before shown such an interest in a suitor in regards to childbearing. Anjou may well have been her last chance to give England an heir, ensure the Tudor dynasty continued, and keep Mary Stuart off the throne. Towards the end of their courtship, his apparent hope that their marriage would produce an heir for his throne and hers showed ignorance of the reality that, by this time, she was most likely beyond conceiving a child. His erotic language and mention of an 'infant Prince of Wales' all seem to suggest that the couple were united and hopeful that their marriage would be granted so they could get to producing an heir without delay.[17] Perhaps his 'burning desire' for Elizabeth was more of an indication of his hopes for an heir for his own kingdom.

By the mid-1560s, Elizabeth's romantic affection for Dudley had already dwindled prior to his scandalous secret marriage to Lettice Knollys. Certainly, at one point, Dudley was the closest person to the queen but the succession question put things into perspective for her. Prior to Mary Stuart's fall from grace, Elizabeth had been on good terms with her cousin, even though she was a Catholic. The English queen was already well into her thirties at this time and without an heir, so Mary would have seemed like the only choice in terms of producing one. Elizabeth may have enjoyed her correspondence with her cousin but she also was suspicious of her overt claims to her throne. She shocked many by offering Dudley, her favourite and rumoured lover, as a husband for Mary. This was prior to her marriage to Darnley, which infuriated Elizabeth. The fact that she offered her favourite to Mary is telling. This way, she could keep an eye on her cousin queen, and control her. Though Mary was a queen, she was a different woman to Elizabeth. It was her belief and everyone else's during this time that, regardless of her position, she was answerable to her husband and God. Thus, Dudley would rule Mary, and Elizabeth would conveniently rule Dudley, as he was her subject. This would have made sense, with her having power over Scotland and England's succession.[18] We now know that these attempts to take some control over her apparent successor failed. Yet, this also shows that she was conscious of the succession, even worried about it, and it shows that she was ever aware of the validity of Mary's claim, whether she was Catholic or not.

Elizabeth was often insecure when it came to Mary Stuart, and the pressure on her to marry throughout most of her reign may not have helped. By the time she came face to face with Anjou, though, she was eager to marry him, and even fell for him. While she was acutely aware that the succession was on the minds of many, and though she had Burghley and a few other minor courtiers on her side, she would have to make her decision on her courtship with Anjou by herself. Thus, she was the orchestrator of her own fate, that of Anjou and Mary, Queen of Scots, and the succession of the crown. Yet, due to all her worries regarding Mary, she had little time to consider the true power she held over the fate of England.

When James VI and I was born, Mary had triumphed over her. Though Elizabeth stated in the past that she wished to remain a virgin, her reaction to the birth of Mary's healthy child, and a boy, is telling. The news was sent to her court and she was told in an informal but discrete way by Burghley. She became enraged to the point where she wished to retire for the evening without dancing. It is said that she lamented to her closest ladies that Mary was 'lighter of a fair son, while she was but barren stock'.[19] Whether this comment was a reflection of her knowledge that she could not bear an heir or simply due to her own situation as a thirty-four-year-old unmarried queen is uncertain. What it does show is that she became increasingly aware that if she wanted to find a husband and produce an heir, she would have to do so soon. It is questionable, therefore, why she waited so long to choose a suitable match. It is possible that Anjou awakened some spark of hope within her that she could find love and produce an heir for England. Until that happened, Mary was forever a thorn in her side, as a woman, as a mother, as a queen, and as her unofficial heir.

Though there were other candidates who had somewhat of a claim to the Tudor throne, Mary Stuart was by far the closest in terms of lineage and royal status. She was Henry VIII's niece, had Tudor and Plantagenet blood, and was already an anointed (yet deposed) queen. Also, she was once queen of France by her first marriage to Anjou's brother, Francis II. All of these factors contributed to Elizabeth's fears regarding the succession. Her subjects were also wary of having a 'foreign' king or queen ruling them one day. The irony in terms of how this relates to Elizabeth's courtship with Anjou perhaps lies in Mary's staunch Catholicism and the fact that she had once been the duke's sister-in-law. Yet, in terms of the succession, Elizabeth did not worry about the consequences of Anjou's religion, as she did with Mary. After all, the duke would only be her consort. Mary, as heir, could initiate, or inspire a Catholic rising to usurp the throne from Elizabeth, who she believed to be the usurper. In the end, she would betray her cousin, and on a number of occasions. This would not only lead to a rift in any relationship they had but also to Mary's demise. Mary's presence in England from the late 1560s possibly influenced Elizabeth's change in mind over marriage, and may have prompted her to open her mind to a match with Anjou. We can never know for sure if Mary's claim to England influenced Elizabeth in this regard but it seems convenient that by the time the queen was heading towards her forties, and without an heir, Mary was more than ready to usurp her throne, and she had an heir.

Due to Mary's valid claims, by 1566, Elizabeth's parliament met to yet again discuss their anxieties over her lack of an heir. They were anxious that she should nominate a successor, or marry, or both. These pleas would not be renewed until as late as 1576, only two years prior to the beginning of negotiations of marriage to the duke. Elizabeth could not agree on the first proposed negotiations in 1572 for a match between two of Catherine de Medici's sons, Anjou included, mainly due to the candidates' youth and religion. Yet, something changed between 1572 and 1579 to make her reconsider the idea of marrying, and Anjou in particular. Was it simply down to chance? Or was it something else? The answer is complex, and we may never truly know for sure. However, it seems that her reasons for opening up talks of marriage again are down to her own insecurities. A more personal reason, as well as a political one, seems rational. Prior to Mary's disgrace and abdication, and before she was forced to flee to England, Elizabeth was already insecure due to her lack of an heir, but also because of her ageing appearance.

In May of 1564, prior to her disgrace, Mary had sent Sir James Melville to visit Elizabeth in an attempt to negotiate their crumbling relationship due to a strain brought on by Mary's claims to the English crown. Melville kept a detailed account of his trip to the English court and it is clear that he paid close attention to Elizabeth's feelings and views towards Mary in terms of the succession and also as a woman. She made it her business to question him on Mary's beauty, stature, and overall grace and accomplishments in comparison to herself. Her insistence that he make comparisons in terms of appearance, height, dancing and musical skills made him uncomfortable and he became anxious to leave early. She also made the mistake of telling him that if she were inclined to marry, she would choose Robert Dudley but, as she was not so inclined, she wished for Mary to take him as her husband.[20]

This mention of her thoughts on marrying Dudley, not only would have startled Melville but would have insulted Mary personally, for it was believed by this time that Dudley and Elizabeth had once been lovers. She mentioned this for a reason, however. With Robert as Mary's husband, she would consider naming her as her heir. We know in hindsight that this was her attempt to control Mary through him, and that Mary was against such a match. What has not been widely considered is that this shows Elizabeth's insecurity as a queen. She feared a Catholic conspiracy to put Mary on her throne so much that she was willing to give up her first real love and closest male companion to counter it. Her pettiness in terms of Mary's appearance can be understood in two ways. One theory is that it was simply due to her own vanity, which some historians have commented on, and many believe that she was jealous, often perplexed by Mary's beauty and courage. Though this seems likely in several ways, it could be that her insecurities went even deeper.

Both women were female monarchs, yet, while Mary acted every bit the queen, or queen consort – marrying a strong man and producing a son – Elizabeth was different. She was every bit the king but in the body of a woman, and was clearly one of the most educated women in Europe, if not the best educated, with a mind as sharp as a razor. Mary had none of this, and though it has often been stated that Elizabeth was incredibly vain, Mary was frivolous, and loved to spend lavishly on her femininity. Elizabeth worried that if it were possible to depose one female monarch, it was also relatively easy for her own countrymen to depose her as queen. Though both women were different as rulers, each was hot-tempered (a Tudor characteristic) and equally as passionate. Elizabeth knew what it was to suffer and be close to damnation – even death. Her father's order of her mother's execution, her warped relationship with Thomas Seymour, and her strained relationship with her sister Mary all took their toll on her state of mind. Yes, the Tudor period was a much more severe period of history in general but that does not mean Elizabeth's anxieties can be dismissed. On the contrary, Mary Stuart gave her much to worry about. Her poor example as a female ruler, and her irrational and devastating decisions in terms of marrying and bearing a child, may well have made Elizabeth even stronger in her opposition to marriage. Yet, by the time Mary was her prisoner, and Catholic conspiracy was becoming ever more fervent in England, she may have reconsidered what it meant to have the protection of a husband, Catholic or not, and the possible security of a male heir.

By the time Lord Darnley was dead and Mary was under English 'protection', Elizabeth, despite Burghley's protests, was not willing to give any more considerations in terms of marrying, nor could she name Mary as her heir. If this frustrated her council, it frustrated Mary even more. Elizabeth was baffled by her cousin's demands, and responded by addressing her care for Mary's state of mind. In 1570, Mary wrote to her:

> In your letter I note a heap of confused, troubled thoughts
> … earnestly and curiously uttered to express your great fear
> and to require of me comfort, concerning both which many
> kinds of speeches are diversely expressed and dispersed in
> your letter, that if I had not consideration that the same did
> proceed from a troubled mind, I might rather take occasion to
> be offended with you than to relent your desires.[21]

It seems that Elizabeth had every reason to fear Mary the prisoner more than Mary the queen. If any rebellions were to succeed in freeing Mary and placing her on Elizabeth's throne, Elizabeth's life would once again be in serious danger. By the late 1570s, Mary was still imprisoned but alive, and Catholic Spain and the rest of Europe were an ever-growing threat to the security of England and Elizabeth's Protestant reign.

Elizabeth may have well been put in a position where she could no longer ignore the fact that she had no child of her own and no husband to help her produce one. Her beloved kingdom was at risk and, ever the dutiful queen, she decided to open up negotiations of marriage with France, who would be a strong ally against Spain. By this time, Anjou was no longer a teenager, and she was acutely aware that, at this point, it did not matter. She had no other foreign suitors, and she would have no other, save Anjou, again. Dudley had betrayed her and was now again married, and Mary, Queen of Scots was hungry for escape and power. Elizabeth saw the convenience in Anjou's desperation to become a king himself. What began as her only means of protecting herself from the treachery of Mary Stuart would become one of the most fascinating courtships in English history. Yet, the true affection that would grow between Elizabeth and Anjou has been widely ignored due to all of these other factors surrounding this courtship. So, without the threat of Mary Stuart, Elizabeth may never have considered a match with the duke, and without him, she may never have considered a last chance at giving England an heir. Thus, in a way, it was Mary who brought Elizabeth and Anjou together.

Chapter 8

On Monsieur's Departure

The Duke of Anjou's faithful second visit to England seemed rather successful initially. Elizabeth and her frog prince had both openly declared their love for each other, and the queen had publically accepted him as the man she wished to marry. Whilst many lamented her 'poor' choice in a consort, many supported her. Though her favourites at court seemed divided, she appeared defiant. Yet, what lay underneath was a scared and uncertain, beyond middle-aged woman. The language in the letters sent between them indicates a more intimate and familiar relationship than has been previously suggested by historians. Indeed, the openness in terms of affection and confirmation of their love, or at least Elizabeth's love, by means of exchanging rings and kisses, is another aspect to consider when discussing the emotions behind this courtship. She knew that Anjou was her last chance to marry, possibly produce an heir, and find someone to share her burden of ruling England. As we know, however, the problem of his religion and the opposition of her subjects as a whole would plague her already fragile and tiring mind. These factors would eventually lead her to make a decision that would not only have an effect on the rest of her life but also perhaps the future of England.

By exchanging rings in public, they were letting their close bond be known, yet what was to come would not only shock Anjou – who probably felt their marriage was imminent – it is likely to have given Elizabeth some much needed relief. So, what changed the queen's mind within such a short period of time? Perhaps she had lain awake all that night, as she usually did, pondering anxiously over her actions and the words she had spoken. Often, she was racked with guilt following a serious decision or the falling out with a favourite, or disagreement with a member of the Privy Council. It is no surprise then that her impulsive language and gestures had stirred a bout of anxiety and doubt in her mind. Perhaps she had simply thought better of her decision or had a discussion with her ladies or Burghley. However, the answer may well be that, though she was sure of her love, or at least affection for Anjou, she became uncertain that he reciprocated those feelings. It seems that his second visit to England, as romantic as his gestures seemed, was more about gaining English funds than about acquiring an English queen. Although it may be true that they shared an intimacy that cannot be overlooked as anything but romantic, the probable reality is that he was more interested in bettering his current position in the Netherlands. Arguments on this theory are conflicting because it seems that there was still some affection left in him for the ageing queen.

With Anjou being more fiscal than romantic during his second visit, Elizabeth would have been aware that keeping up the appearance that this was a love match on both sides was an important task. Though she would have been full of anxiety concerning the duke's true agenda, she knew she could not be blamed for the breakdown of Anglo-French political relations if he decided to retract from the marriage negotiations. The demanding conditions her council put forward to the French in terms of religion, power, and how the marriage would work overall put the pressure on, and it became acutely obvious that the duke, and the French as a whole, would soon want to back out of the talks. These demands would have been seen as absurd to the French commissioners involved due to their staunch Catholic observance and intentions to make better of France's power in this matter of marriage.[1]

If Elizabeth was unsure as to whether Anjou's feelings had altered, or if his obligations had changed, she wanted it to appear that they were still going to marry. This would at least keep the Anglo-French alliance alive a while longer and give her more time to think on the matter of foreign policy, and also what to do about the still-existing threat to England's security. Anjou became increasingly impatient with her after the dramatic exchanging of rings in front of the whole court and French diplomat, and after receiving England's terms and conditions for the proposed marriage. This behaviour would not have sat well with the queen, who liked to ponder for a time before making decisions on matters of state. It seems that, though they were alike in many ways, they were also different, and had separate agendas by this point. Henry III, the duke's brother, wrote that he would not support Elizabeth's defence against the Spanish if she did not marry his brother. The pressure was again thrust upon her to make a decision, and, for a time, it did seem that she was adamant to marry him.[2]

She had to remain stealthy in how she proceeded. It is said that the day after she gave the ring to Anjou and openly declared that they would marry, she realized she could never really give him what he wanted and, if she wanted to hold onto any power at all, she had to submit to the will of her people and call off marriage negotiations once and for all. Whether she did let the duke down the next day or not is subject to interpretation. While she may have been under so much pressure that she could no longer take the strain, it must also be noted that she was well used to keeping her suitors at arm's length to suit her own political agenda. Though she may have loved the duke, there were more important things than her own happiness. If her people were to oppose the marriage entirely, who was to say they wouldn't revolt? In this regard, the forced abdication of her cousin, Mary, Queen of Scots, would not have been far from her mind. Mary's poor choices in terms of husbands, foreign policy, and matters of religion had all led her to her current, dire situation as a prisoner in a foreign land. Elizabeth had to avoid this at all costs.

Despite best efforts by both parties, it became evident to

them that their marriage would never come about. Regardless of when she told the duke that she could not marry him – when the words eventually came to her, the duke seemed genuinely aggrieved and shocked. Yet, he must have known prior to his sailing to England that religious and political matters would most likely bring an end to their courtship. Both of them kept up appearances in public, and though she had made her final decision on the matter, the duke remained in England for some months after. Whether or not this was to keep the Anglo-French alliance strong for as long as possible as a favour to Elizabeth, or due to his hopes that she would change her mind and marry him upon impulse is not clear. The 'lovers' pose' was still the centre of court attention and gossip, whilst keeping up appearances was probably in the best interests of both Elizabeth and Anjou to save them any embarrassment. Though the duke seemed outwardly contented with the queen's decision, he was overheard 'cursing the lightness of women in general, and the perfidy of islanders in particular'. It is clear that he was deeply unhappy at the prospect of not becoming England's king-consort, yet whether this was due to the loss of the kingdom, or the queen in particular, is unknown.[3]

The true emotional value of their letters indicates that they were in favour of marrying, and yet, though this interpretation is contrary to most modern viewpoints, the consequences of Elizabeth's decision to end the courtship are also a testament to the very real love that once existed between a prince and a queen. The fact that the duke remained in England is also a hint of his hopes that they may have rekindled their courtship. Whether or not his greed overtook his true affections for the queen is of little importance in the overall evaluation of their feelings for one another. Elizabeth's feelings, expressed in her own hand, along with her almost betraying mind over matter, is a further indication that she felt deep affection for Anjou. Evidently, her decision to end the courtship was necessary, yet the emotions and regrets that she would experience later on in her life show us the real woman behind the iconography of Elizabeth the 'Virgin Queen'. There would also be dire consequences to her decision to end the courtship in terms of her reputation. Certainly, the queen would never be offered the hand of a foreign prince or king again, and she would remember her last courtship with great regret, a melancholic fondness, and yearning. This may have been the greatest tragedy of her life.

She explained to the duke that she loved him but the opposition of her people meant that her conscience could not allow for their marriage to take place. They may have agreed to keep up appearances at court to save face. Or, perhaps she worried that she may yet again change her mind? The answer may simply be that this was a political tactic to give England more time. By now, she would have been sure that England had no choice but to eventually go to war with Spain. This is probably why she offered him payment. She initially gave him a sum of ten thousand pounds, with the promise that he would receive a further fifty thousand. This may well have been her way of bribing him to leave England. Philippa Jones is of this impression.[4] However, though Elizabeth may well have worried that the duke's continued presence at her court would bring about more doubts on her part, it is far more likely that she was using the payment as a means to ensure his loyalty to her personally and to England. This would mean that she could count on his support and, if necessary, his army if Spain were to attempt an invasion of England. While Anjou did not get exactly what he wanted – to become England's king – he agreed to the terms of payment to support his cause in the Netherlands and the war against Spain.

Though their courtship was over, his stay in England for a couple of months after her decision may have worked to ease tensions between them, and by the time he was set to sail, a sadness seemed to overwhelm Elizabeth. However, even though the pair continued to write to one another, still claiming their undying affection, the tone had somewhat changed, with the relationship now more about the political than the romantic. She still needed France in terms of an ally, and Anjou relied on her in terms of financial support.

The money she had to pay in order to keep him happy, along with his insistence on staying in England longer than was necessary or expected, is a testimony to his true character. Whether or not he truly loved her at some point did not matter now – he had failed in his endeavour to marry a queen and gain a true kingdom of his own. The notion that Elizabeth decided within the timeframe of one night that she had made a feckless error in openly declaring her intention to marry Anjou could carry some merit. It was reported that, on the night of 22nd November, she was plagued and tormented by her indecision, clearly distraught at having to decide on the love of her people or the love of Anjou. The fact that she had also stated in front of a French diplomat that she would marry the duke probably did nothing to help her anxieties. Her ladies are said to have been in 'floods of tears', begging her to reflect on her decision to marry and consider the hazards of childbirth at her age. While her ladies' words may have helped her in coming to a decision, she ultimately made her mind up by herself. She was the queen, after all, and it was her decision, as outlined by her council.[5]

Yet, the duke would prove to be stubborn in his response to her ending of the courtship. Many believe this is due to his loss of a crown. But what of his emotional attachment to Elizabeth? Surely this was a loss to him also? The question for her council was now of Anjou's departure. They had gotten what they wanted with the queen informing the duke that she could not marry him. His reaction is telling. Clearly embarrassed by her change of heart, he became determined to make her pay. Though it may seem that this was in wait of a bribe for him to leave, which he got, he also may have hoped she might change her mind once again, for she was known to change her mind at the last minute regarding many matters. This is clear from some of the letters she wrote to him during their early courtship. The queen would write of her feelings, have the letter dispatched, then recall it at the last minute. So, to Anjou, it was possible that if he stayed on long enough for her to grow used to his presence, she might well have a change of heart. This was not to be, however, with Elizabeth adhering to her final decision.[6]

His hopes that she would change her mind if he paraded himself around her court, seemly as the devoted suitor, would have the opposite effect. She soon became fed up with his presence, which would have become as embarrassing as it did intolerable. His stubbornness was something she had not witnessed before. Nor had she expected his reaction to the ending of their courtship to be so dramatic. He displayed public scenes, ranting that he would kill himself or carry her away by force. Though she may not have taken his threats seriously, she knew that the longer he stayed at her court, displaying dramatic scenes of the jilted groom, the more attention he would draw from foreign courts. As necessary as it was for her to refuse him in the end, she must have known that her final decision would be followed by gossip. Though the loss of the duke as her final potential husband was a hard blow to take, the sniggers of the Parisians was an even harder pill to swallow. In November, a caricature of her on horseback was pinned up all over the city, displaying her with her dress slightly raised by her right hand. A figure of Anjou was also depicted in this scene, with a hawk on his wrist. The hawk is symbolic of his failed attempts to gain her hand. The man who engraved this image was a Catholic named Richard Verstegen, who was a propagandist for the Guise family.[7] Clearly, this was not only embarrassing for her, it also meant that she was drawn into other political situations she would never have dared to imagine. Perhaps she felt that, in letting Anjou down, she had saved herself from a future of ridicule such as this.

In making a final decision, she was expressing her true role as a monarch, willing to put the needs of her subjects and country before her own desires, and though this may be interpreted as weakness or insecurity, it can also be regarded as an example of her courage, strength, and true leadership. Her decision was due to religion and therefore separated Elizabeth the queen from Elizabeth the woman. Elizabeth Tudor, the woman, may have loved the Duke of Anjou, but Elizabeth Regina, the queen and God's representative on Earth of the Protestant Faith, loved the English people more. When analyzing her earlier letters to Anjou, it is clear that she saw no point in further negotiation regarding marriage because he was resolute in his intentions to express his religion openly: '…unless it pleases you to make other resolution other than the open exercise of religion, and it seems good to you to write to me about it or to send some good answer; for I desire nothing that does not content you.'[8] This suggests that Elizabeth clearly knew from as early as 1580 that she would not be able to accomplish anything in the matter of marriage to Anjou, if he did not realise the pressure she was under due to his religion. Here, she made her feelings to him known from the beginning.

Her feelings towards him were now wearing thin. It became increasingly difficult for her to pretend any longer, and her irritation at his presence grew. She may have still loved him but, no matter how much she tried to reassure him that her decision was down to politics and religion rather than a lack of personal feelings, he remained determined as ever. He was hurt by her apparent eagerness for his departure, and though it may seem that he was after some form of compensation, as many historians have suggested, the reality is likely more complicated than this.[9]

By 1582, her greatest courtship was over. She accompanied Anjou to Canterbury for his departure back to the Netherlands. They openly displayed their grief and were said to have been in tears. Some have suggested that this was Elizabeth using political theatre, even faking a display of grief to give those who witnessed the event of the duke's departure a show. Yet, their shared sadness may have been genuine. Whether or not this is due to their undying love for one another, or the loss of the chance to marry and produce an heir to both their crowns, is speculative. As their story did not necessarily end with his departure from England, it could be suggested that they did care for one another, even loved each other, despite the disastrous end to their courtship. It is possible that her feelings towards his eventual departure were the result of a combination of factors, including the loss of political influence in Europe and protection against the Spanish, vengeance against Dudley, the desire for an heir and, notably, the loss of a chance at love.[10] It is likely, as it is evident when it comes to human nature, that her decision and its consequences were more complex than previously thought.

Reports of her true feelings regarding Anjou's departure vary. Some mention her in floods of tears as he sailed off, never to return. The French Ambassador described the queen as 'tearful and regretful', openly displaying her grief with a hint of pride and pleasure. Certainly, it seems that she basked in the melancholy resulting from the duke's final departure.[11] Was this some strange longing to be a true widow rather than the virgin queen who dismissed her last chance at love, or a ruse to keep the French as a keen ally and friend? Other reports, like that from the Spanish ambassador, state that she danced with glee around her bedchamber 'for every joy of getting rid of him'.[12]

Elizabeth's own feelings regarding the departure of her frog prince are evident in a poem entitled 'On Monsieur's Departure', which she probably wrote in 1582, either just before or just after the duke's departure. Here she clearly expresses her grief:

I grieve, and dare not show my discontent;
I love, and yet am forced to seem to hate;
I dote, yet dare not say I ever meant;
I seem stark mute, yet inwardly do prate.
I am and am not – Freeze, and yet I burn,
Since from myself my other self I turn.
My care is like my shadow in the sun –
Follows me flying, flies when I pursue it...[13]

The poem is extraordinarily personal, and shows the true depth of her grief over the loss of Anjou. Many have stated that this may have been political, or simply an amalgamation of feelings regarding her position as a female ruler and a woman who wished to love, yet she has no reason to keep up appearances any longer and it is doubtful that this poem describes any loss other than that of Anjou. Its reference to him cannot be mistaken.

This poem clearly summarizes the queen's lamentations over the implications of her position as monarch. To keep her people happy, and to seem the just and effective female ruler, her true feelings over the ending of the courtship had to be kept private. As Tracy Borman put it perfectly, she had to disguise 'her private desires behind the public face of monarchy'.[14] These few lines also indicate a much more complex individual than has been previously thought. Here, she shows the conflict between her mind and heart, and although, in hindsight, we know that she probably made the right decision, she would have to live with doubts regarding this for the rest of her life and reign. She was evidently an individual who craved love, not just for the queen she was but for the woman underneath. Anjou presented that opportunity once, yet the many obstacles meant their relationship could never prosper the way they had hoped. The queen could not reconcile her many needs, nor could she place her commitment to a man she loved over her commitment to her duty and her people.[15]

Both would continue to write to one another in reference to light affection rather than that of deep desire and true love. Yet, this can be seen as evidence of how genuine their love once was. Though the marriage was off and their feelings would alter somewhat, they could never have imagined that they would never cross paths again. Elizabeth's poetry may be reflective of her regrets regarding the loss of Anjou as a potential husband but her words also offer meditation as well as loss and grief. With her once-imagined future as a bride and possibly a mother now gone, her position as the last Tudor monarch was clear for all to see. Her defense against her council's insistence that she marry would become something of the past, and she could now look to a different kind of reign. While Anjou's departure brought her great sorrow, it would also bring about great victory.[16]

In terms of understanding why she chose her people and her role as queen over love and matrimony, it cannot be doubted that her decision was influenced by the great opposition to her. However, in terms of laying the blame, which many historians have attempted to put on her Privy Council and the men around her, it must be noted that her council could not have acted against her wishes as queen. Therefore, this contradicts recent interpretations that she had no role in policy-making, particularly foreign policy. On the contrary, she took an active part in many if not all stages of policy-making, including that of her marriage negotiations to Anjou. Therefore, the blame cannot solely lie with the men she surrounded herself with. It must also be remembered that she chose to surround herself with men who were likeminded in terms of her views, and she took their advice seriously, despite her own feelings and emotions.[17]

In every regard, Elizabeth had precedence over the Privy Council. She received all relative information directly, took a serious interest in the minor details of negotiations, and heeded the counsel offered to her by those both against and for the marriage. So, though it may seem that she was an over-emotional and indecisive character, she was also a shrewd politician and diplomat. This does not mean her emotions and affections towards Anjou were false or a tactic but, rather, she was willing to listen to the advice given to her if those around her were willing to listen to her. If anyone was to blame for the end of what would be her final courtship, her last chance to marry, to possibly (though unlikely) have a child and give England an heir, it was the queen herself. Along with the many meetings with members of the council she trusted and favoured, like Burghley, Sussex, Walsingham, and even Dudley, she also depended on the opinions of lesser-known individuals from the council, such as Wilson and Hundson. These meetings were key in coming to a conclusion over the proposed marriage and, therefore, she probably knew from the beginning of Anjou's second visit that she had to make the decision as a queen, not a woman.

The bad dreams, insomnia, and general melancholic mood she expressed throughout the duke's final stay could also indicate feelings of guilt for having already made a decision privately. She may have placed court and council favourites in charge of the marriage talks because she wished them to come to a conclusion that would give her what she wanted and also guarantee that her feelings towards Anjou were respected. There is also no reason to believe that the council formed by her was anything but honest and genuine in their decision to allow her to marry whom she chose. Though, it is clear from events later on in her reign that, in terms of national security, the council could put such pressure on her that their verdict would end up being the final say. This is true in terms of the execution of Mary, Queen of Scots, for example. While the council did not wish to go against their queen, it seems that they pushed her into action when the occasion was necessary. Therefore, neither Elizabeth nor her council was entirely to blame for her final decision. The end of the courtship was inevitable, and based on so many factors that it would never have ended well for them as a couple, married or not.[18]

Elizabeth could also be hypocritical when it came to the marriage of courtiers. During her reign, many marriages that were arranged in secret were born out of mutual love and desire. She found this intolerable, growing furious towards such marriages after her courtship with Anjou had ended. It is well known that she could display an unusually bad temper towards her attendants, council members, and court in general. She treated sexual indiscretion and secret marriages seriously and offered many forms of punishment for both parties, often including their families. Such venomous reactions to marriages based on mutual affection became so well known throughout England and Europe that many of her courtiers feared ever revealing their secret nuptials, even after it had produced several children. The queen's hypocritical reactions to illicit affairs and secret marriages, such as that of Dudley and Lettice Knollys, have contributed to the existing historiography surrounding her reign, particularly towards the end of her life. However, many have considered Robert Dudley to blame for this due to his betrayal. Never has it been considered that Elizabeth's later venom was down to the fact that she could not marry the man she wished, or that she would never get the chance to marry again.[19]

The queen was not angry with love in general. As mentioned previously, she was willing to accept couples' petitions to marry once her permission was sought, and once she found them to be a suitable match. Therefore, it would have made little sense to exclude her from any knowledge of a courtship. This is where the existing historiography of her later reign must be re-evaluated and challenged, as it depicts a one-sided version of her that does not allow for further insight into her emotions. If her courtship with the duke and the many letters and displays of affection cannot conclude that she was in love with him, and he perhaps with her (for a time), then her reaction to his departure, subsequent letters and reaction to his death certainly can. Losing the duke as a potential husband and lover was one thing but losing him entirely would prove such a blow to her personally that she would never truly recover from it. The next two years of her life would bring great tragedy, yet her reserve and courage were ever present. With the brewing storm ahead brought on by the Spanish, and the loss of her 'frog' prince, the queen would need all the courage she could muster.

Chapter 9

The Extremity of My Misfortune

When Anjou left England on 1st February 1582, both he and Elizabeth had no inclination that they would ever see each other again. Even so, though their courtship was over, their correspondence continued. In hindsight, she must have felt quite the failure. She knew her last chance at love and marriage was finally lost but also that the alliance with France would probably crumble. Whether she and Anjou kept up correspondence out of love or for political gain is uncertain. However, on close inspection of her letters after the duke's departure, though somewhat cooler, the language and familiarity indicates that the spark between the two had not vanished entirely. After some time, she may well have regretted her final decision to call off the courtship, yet she would never have admitted it openly.

Letters began to fly back and forth between them almost immediately. However, the tone of the letters regarding political matters and the duke's payment, which she had not yet fully granted, is different to that of the letters from their early and mid-courtship. On 24th May, she wrote to him from Greenwich. She opens her letter as she always had, addressing him as her 'dearest', showing her gratitude for his previous letters and his willingness to respond to her, considering how they parted and how busy he would have been in his endeavours in the Netherlands. Whether her words were at this stage sincere or not is open to interpretation, yet it must be noted that, by the time the courtship ended and life began to return to 'normal' for her, she had no need to use such language. In terms of keeping up the appearance of an alliance, she would not have needed to use such familiarity: 'You make me acknowledge that notwithstanding the great affairs and importance of your business, you fail not to console me with the coming of your long writings, and for them confessing myself infinitely obliged to you.'[1]

Though she is not using romantic language here per se, she is using a familiarity the duke would recognize. It could be argued that she was pining for him, though it seems unlikely that she was still in a state of grief three months after his return to the Netherlands.

She continues to comment on the duke's obvious affection in his letters and that she can see 'humours of several qualities'. However, when she mentions that it pleased Anjou 'to tell me at length, the hazards, losses, and machinations that you have endured for my sake', it could be said that this is an indication of his expressed frustration with her decision to end the courtship. Indeed, she is careful to lament her decisions, without actually apologizing or having to change her mind. She states that she could never forget and that the memories are 'engraved in my soul, where, until its separation from my body, I will not leave to recognize and be pained by them always.'[2] The way she expressed herself in this letter implies that her feelings for Anjou were not only genuine in hindsight but it also shows her regret in encouraging him, only to let him down on more than one occasion. It is also indicative from her reply that the duke still had some affection for her. Or perhaps this is due to her not having paid him the remaining 50,000 pounds yet. Regardless, it seems likely that there were regrets on both sides about how their courtship ended.

Here, she is careful to remind him that though she feels some guilt and much sadness for how they parted, she is not entirely to blame. She insists that any postponements of negotiations or a wedding were out of her control, and though we know that the decision was down to her, she may be referring to the matter of the duke's religion and the French stance on the Privy Council's earlier conditions: '…I entreat you not to forget that all these postponements have not derived from me, my thoughts not having been lacking in respect of our more happy stay in this country...'[3] And she continues: 'Remove, therefore, my dearest Monsieur, any thought that I stand to blame for the passion of anger that gives you offense because your constancy should be doubted.'[4]

This is a pretty heavy tone, compared to that of her past letters to him. She clearly indicates that though he remains courteous and claims his continued affection for her in his letters, he can no longer hide his anger or frustration regarding their failed attempts to marry. This frustration was, however, evident in his previous letters in 1579/80. Yet, it was typical of Elizabeth on many occasions to take the blame away from herself, and place it on others.

She mentions letters from the king and queen (most likely Catherine, the Queen Mother) of France, and apologizes for her lack of a quick reply, despite the ambassador reminding her several times, and she is clear to mention that the king has the right to repute her for this lack of hasty reply. This suggests that she became more relaxed regarding the French alliance once she had made it clear that she would not marry Anjou. Yet, it also seems that the French, particularly Catherine, were unhappy with the outcome of the negotiations and were becoming increasingly frustrated with her. If she would not marry the French heir, then what use was she? What could France benefit from an alliance with England? Elizabeth promises to resolve these issues and goes into the topic of money, which clearly shows that the duke had inquired as to its whereabouts in his previous letter. She is clever to absolve herself from any blame regarding the lack of funds, using her femininity as an excuse, indicating that the fault lies with those who take charge of her finances: 'If you bring up the subject of money, I am so poor as an orator for my profit and like so little to play the housewife that I give charge of this to such that are wiser than I.'

At this point, she had clearly changed her tune. Though she may still have held affection for the duke, she was not willing to send him a large sum of English money but nor could she openly deny what she had promised. This is a tactic she used for most of her life – play the helpless and feeble woman – and surely she could not be blamed. However, Anjou was no longer willing to play the courteous suitor for fear that she would reject him. The queen states that her inability to send funds at that time did not mean she lacked support for the duke's endeavours: '...you will see that I do not have less consideration of your greatness and contentation in your enterprises than you yourself would be able to wish.'[5] She may well have loved Anjou but was also clearly well informed of his failure in his given position in the Netherlands. Though they continued to speak on matters of marriage and romance, as well as matters of politics and finances, she could never have funded such a poorly capable ruler.

While he was happily playing tennis in Antwerp, his soldiers were beginning to grow unhappy and there was even talk of mutiny. Eventually, the threat to his life would become more serious than he could have ever imagined. His military campaigns were clearly unpopular and expensive. He had probably run out of funds long before he was forced to flee, and Elizabeth's lack of financial help would have played a role in this. Yet, she knew she could not involve herself in his unpopular campaigns. Despite her feelings, she was proving that she would remain an effective ruler, and never consider her own country's safety and security as inferior to that of her heart. She touches on her feelings in her letter to Anjou from the end of May, reminding him to remember the affection they both once shared: 'Do not forget my heart, which I risk a little for you in this matter – more than you will be able to imagine but not more than I already feel.'[6]

Though she also mentions the sum of money here, which the duke brought up in his letter, she is careful to note that her feelings for him remain the same but will not grow deeper. This may be in referral to the money, which she is cleverly trying to avoid sending. Her reference to the duke's 'commission', which she does state 'we will give you' is indicative of her strategy in keeping up appearances. Even if she did still have feelings for him, she was not prepared to seriously contemplate parting with such a sum of money for a man she could not marry. The existing copy of this letter breaks off at this point where she mentions money, so the conclusion can only be left to speculation. However, it must be noted that Anjou never received the remaining sum promised him by the queen.[7]

By the end of 1583, it is clear that the once-undeniable affection between Elizabeth and her frog prince was fading. Though they continued to write to one another, her language had changed – her tone utterly cooled. Also, the duke seems to have continued to pressure her to fund his military campaigns in the Netherlands. Henry III, the French king, and his mother, Catherine de Medici, were also mounting pressure on Elizabeth to intervene, yet they themselves seemed reluctant to take full responsibility for Anjou's failures. The queen became increasingly frustrated, and her letter to him on 10th September 1583 clearly outlines her sentiments. She opens by addressing him as 'Monsieur', rather than the typical 'dearest', though she begins lightly by referring to the visit of Monsieur de Reaux to the English court, and the duke's many letters indicating his continued affection for her. However, she is quick to get into the matter of what de Reaux had actually reported to her regarding Anjou's state of affairs: '...I have heard of the care that you take for fear of some bad impression that I could conceive of your actions.'[8]

Her feelings are clear from the beginning, and she is obviously on the defensive. It would seem likely that, by this point, any illusion regarding the long, lost love between them had now faded. If anything, she began to feel like a mother rather than a lover. She continues in her letter on the point of de Reaux's report: 'He tired me with language that seemed very strange to me: that you desire to know what will be the aid you will give for the preservation of the Netherlands...'[9] Her frustration with the duke's continued demands are clear when she mentions that his begging will do him no good in terms of their alliance or friendship: '…how unfortunate you are to believe that this is the way to preserve your friends, by always debilitating them!'[10]

The advice the duke is receiving, she states, is clearly indicative of a person who does not favour their 'friendship' and alliance. She is not only reprimanding Anjou for his behaviour but openly giving him counsel, which he clearly had no mind to take. Then she is careful to remind him that she has other alliances – 'friends' – and duties to consider other than him. The tone here is clearly different to that of their earlier letters, which hinted at their hopes and desires. She also indicates that she does not possess unlimited funds, although her use of language to indicate this is somewhat difficult to make out: 'You will not esteem me so unworthy of reigning that I may fortify myself, indeed, with the sinews of war'.[11] The 'sinews of war' she mentions here refers to unlimited money.

Her complaints about the duke's brother, the king, are also made clear throughout this letter, and it may be that she blamed him for Anjou's actions and poor judgement. She states that she is 'astonished by the king, our brother, who has given me the precedence in fortifying you in so great a need'.[12] Not only is the king leaving the difficult task of funding the duke's failing endeavours to Elizabeth, France was also in a much more comfortable financial position than England at this time. She is quick to take control of her feelings, however, and states that if Anjou and his brother, the king, continue to insist that she sends financial aid to the Netherlands, then she will have no other option but to end their alliance.[13] She also comments on Anjou's contrary nature and his changing moods. The man being revealed to her now was far from the doting young prince eager to woo her, and she must have wondered if his feelings were ever genuine. She may well have felt glad that she ended their courtship before it was too late.

She takes care to warn Anjou of his judgements and attitude. Whether this is in terms of their relationship or how he conducts business and runs his state is unclear, yet, nonetheless, she advises: 'I hope among other things that you will remember that he is well worthy of falling into nets: do not only take advice, think shrewdly – that is enough'.[14] Her final paragraph indicates that she wishes for the duke, along with the king and queen mother of France, to lessen their harsh judgment of her. Clearly, she is indicating that she has no desire to send aid to Anjou, regardless of the insistence of the French. She asks him to do right by her, implying that she still had some faith in his good nature. Her closing is emotional and confrontational, reminding the duke of her love for him, whilst also remembering to play the victim: '…I will never cease honouring, loving and esteeming you like the dog who, often beaten, returns to his master'. The language at the end of the letter is strong and telling. She is careful to remind the duke of her affections, though it seems that, at this point, any true love she felt for him is slowly but surely being replaced with frustration and contempt.

The Duke of Anjou embarked on several military campaigns during the early 1580s. When he became ill on his final campaign, which was failing, anyway, he withdrew his forces and returned to Paris. By the time he returned to his homeland, he was disgraced, generally unpopular, and was so ill that he seemed to be slowly wasting away. Shortly before this, Elizabeth had asked John Dee to foretell the duke's future. Clearly, she had enough care and affection left for the duke that she thought to ask her astrologer for his help. Dee told her that Anjou would commit suicide, and though he may have been wrong in how his demise came about, the suddenness of it was correct. Elizabeth would not have known that the duke was ill at this time, nor would she have been in contact with him for some time due to the movement of his military campaign. It cannot be said for certain what ailed Anjou but many historians have diagnosed malaria as the cause of death. Certainly, he would have suffered from weight loss and fever, amongst other reported ailments that can be attributed to the condition. Thus, it seems likely that this was the case.[15]

He died on 10th June 1584, barely thirty years old. Elizabeth was now fifty, and beyond the point of ever marrying or conceiving a child. The link to her last chance to fulfill her most important duty was now gone. Everyone at court feared telling her the sad news. There would have been no good time to inform her, and when it happened, she is said to have wept uncontrollably, ordered her court into mourning, and wore black for three weeks. Interestingly, though many historians state that any love she may have had for Anjou was completely gone by the time he died, her reaction is telling as to how she really felt. The queen reportedly sobbed openly, at random, and for a long period of time after the duke's death. She even observed the anniversary of his death every year until she, too, died.[16] While she would continue to have her favourites, none would ever match that of the duke in terms of affection or dedication. She continued to keep the company of Dudley, yet it would never be the same, and she was always reminded of his betrayal. The Duke of Anjou, however, for all his flaws and demands, never betrayed her trust, and the fact that they kept contact until his death is indicative of their shared affection, regardless of their problems.

Though she had abandoned the idea of ever marrying Anjou, her reaction to his death seems one of genuine loss. Inside her prayer book she used for private devotion, there can be seen two immature figures by Hillard: that of the queen herself, and one of Anjou. This item would have been personal to the queen, and rarely seen by others. Therefore, the fact that she had it commissioned is indicative of her true feelings for the duke, and her sadness for the loss of him in terms of their courtship and his death. She wore the book around her waist for the rest of her life, attached by a girdle. It has been noted that it was one of her most precious possessions until she died.[17]

If her public display of mourning for the duke is not convincing enough of the affection, even love she once held for him, then her private letter to Catherine de Medici certainly is. The letter, which is addressed to Catherine as 'To Madame, my good sister the queen mother', is intimate, truthful, and displays a side to Elizabeth that she rarely felt comfortable showing. Clearly, this letter was for the eyes of Catherine only. It was probably written during the period of Elizabeth's deep mourning, where her court had to follow suit. The letter itself was originally written in French, in the queen's own hand, and though its existence offers a greater insight into her grief and feelings for Anjou, it remains in a rather fragile state, the paper badly worn. The way in which she addresses the French queen as her 'good sister' is not something unusual in her letters to other royals. She often wrote to Mary Stuart, addressing her as her 'sister', and ironically would address Mary's son, James VI, as her 'dear brother'.[18] Her tone is clearly mournful from the beginning of the letter, and Catherine would have had no confusion as to its intentions. This was not only Elizabeth expressing her condolences to the woman who may well have been her mother-in-law, it was also probably a political tactic to keep any alliance with France going as long as possible. Regardless of this factor, however, her genuine feeling of loss for the duke cannot be dismissed here, and it seems that she would have felt some comfort, even closeness to the duke, in writing to his mother. She begins:

> If the extremity of my unhappiness had not equaled my grief for his sake and had not rendered me inadequate to touch with pen the wound that my heart suffers, it would not be possible that I would have so forgotten myself as not to have visited you in the company that I make with you in your sorrow, which I am sure cannot be greater than my own.[19]

Here, she is not only expressing her condolences for the duke's death but also her regret and sorrow in general for her own personal loss of him. The language is tellingly emotional, reflecting the truth behind her grief. It may seem that his death brought up regrets regarding the ending of their courtship, and a guilt in having allowed her last chance at love to slip away so easily. Whatever the case, she seems genuine in her mourning. She is also boldly implying that her grief, if not the same as Catherine's, is even greater. Certainly, she is suggesting that the duke's own mother's grief could in no way outweigh hers. This may have been on purpose, as an attempt to convince Catherine of the true nature of her feelings for Anjou, and though it may have been for political reasons, it seems more likely that this is her way of reaching out, and wishing to share the loss of the duke.

If Catherine was shocked by Elizabeth's exclamation that her sorrow was greater than that of her as Anjou's mother, she would find an explanation on the next line: 'For inasmuch as you are his mother, so it is that there remain to you several other children. But for me, I find no consolation except death, which I hope will soon reunite us.'[20]

Elizabeth's explanation for her grief is clear. In stating that her sorrow for the duke's death outweighs that of his mother's because Catherine had many other children to place her affection on, she was perhaps minutely untactful. The language indicates the genuineness of the letter, and the way in which Elizabeth expresses herself is not that of a queen who wishes to continue a political alliance but of a woman who needs to vent her grief and anger, possibly to the only other person who was as close to Anjou as she felt. It may seem that she is attempting to strike a competition in grief, yet this was probably not her intention. At this stage, she knew she would never experience love and longing for marriage again in the way she did for Anjou. She may well have regretted their parting and how it was conducted but her words of sorrow give no hint that she would have ever changed her mind if he had lived. Rather, they reveal the frustration she experienced due to her position in life, without which she may not have had the chance to court the duke.

The queen's statement that she could only find consolation in death with the duke may seem dramatic, yet, it must be noted that prior to Anjou's death, she was already suffering from what can only be described as a form of depression, anxiety, and insomnia. Though applying modern terms and diagnosis to the lives and ailments of past figures should be avoided, it must be noted that whatever way her state of mind is interpreted, the death of Anjou would not have helped. She continues her display of grief, offering Catherine a description of her heart, and stating that her body is without a soul: 'Madame, if you were able to see the image of my heart, you would see the portrait of a body without a soul.'[21]

How she chose to express herself in this letter is significant in relation to confirming the genuineness of her grief. To mention her own feelings in such an intimate manner, with a woman she had never met, nor would ever meet, suggests there was truth in her words. Though she and Anjou may have parted on rather poor terms, and their letters after his departure show strain on the relationship and frustration on both parts, it is evident that the true affection behind the many obstacles placed in front of the couple never truly left, for Elizabeth, anyway.

She further implies that she wishes to extend the love she once had for Anjou to his brother the king and to Catherine herself. Though this may be down to political necessity, it also seems that she was again attempting to make amends for her decision in 1581, and to find a closeness to the duke's family to bring her comfort. It could be that she wished to maintain any relationship between England and France in the form of a family connection, and though that could no longer be through marriage, she insisted that Catherine would find her 'the most faithful daughter and sister that ever princes had'.[22] The mention of 'daughter' clearly refers to Catherine, while 'sister' relates to the king. This is Elizabeth's way of stating that, though she and Anjou never married, she regards his family in the same manner as if they had. It almost would seem that the language in which she chose to express her grief was a deliberate attempt to display herself as a widow. Certainly, her decision to dress in black and order her court into mourning reflects this theory. The assumption could be made that, while she may never have had the chance to play the part of Anjou's bride, she was damned if she was going to dismiss the opportunity of portraying herself as his widow. All of these factors are further indications of her true feelings for him.

Her mention of the duke's closeness to Catherine – 'he belonged to you so nearly, he whom I was entirely dedicated' – is also reminiscent of the words of a widow. She also writes that if the duke had lived longer, she was sure Catherine and the king would have sent him 'more help'. This implies that the king and his mother had sent Anjou inadequate aid and finances for his military endeavours in the Netherlands. This could be taken as Elizabeth subtly blaming them for the duke's failures in that regard, and possibly his untimely death. While this may seem harsh, it was a subtle enough way for her to express her emotions. It is also indicative of her wish to distance herself from the duke's military campaigns and her attempt to dismiss any blame on her part for the consequences of her lack of financial aid. She closes the letter by stating that her thoughts are with the queen mother and that she intends to remain faithful to her 'as if I were your own daughter born'.[23] Then she signs off as 'your very affectionate sister and cousin'. The intention behind the letter is obvious. It is as much about Elizabeth's true feelings for the duke – her regrets about their separation and her grief from his death – as it is about political necessity. England was still threatened by the powerful Spanish, and was thus in need of a strong ally. She could no longer use her feelings for the duke to her political gain, so a display of her mourning was not only necessary in terms of her grief but also for the safety of England.

She seems to have been sincere in her sorrow for Anjou's death, having come so close to marrying him, and they had both enjoyed their courtship, along with the splendour and drama it evoked.[24] The way in which he dedicated himself to her as a woman as well as a queen may have been everything she wished to find in a suitable husband. Perhaps this is why he was the only man she ever entertained in his pursuit of marriage. Though their courtship had come to an end, their continued letters offered her a reminder of the possibilities, and the hope that she once harbored to marry and have a child. Her frog would no longer be there to send her sweet letters of reassurance that she could be loved for herself as well as her crown. Though Anjou undoubtedly began his suit of her for power and position, it seems that their mutual affection for each other would grow where it was thought no seed existed. Elizabeth's final suitor and chance of true love were gone, with a part of her dying with him. A poem written by her in the 1580s, entitled 'When I was fair and young', not only reveals her regret at having never married, the last verse could be taken as a reference to the ending of their courtship, and Anjou's tragic, subsequent death:

When I was fair and young, and favour graced me,
Of many was I sought unto, their mistress for to be.
But did I scorn the all, and said to them therefore,
'Go, go, go seek some otherwhere; importune me no more.

But there fair Venus' son, that brave, victorious boy,
Said, 'What, though scornful dame, sith that thou art so coy,
I will so wound thy heart, that thou shalt learn therefore:
Go, go, go seek some otherwhere; importune me no more.'

But then I felt straightaway a change within my breast:
The day unquiet was; the night I could not rest,
For I did sore repent that I had said before,
'Go, go, go seek some otherwhere; importune me no more.[25]

Chapter 10

All My Husbands

The existing historiography surrounding the courtship of Elizabeth I and the Duke of Anjou has long been in need of re-evaluation. Though it is generally accepted that the queen used the Anglo-French alliance as a means of political strategy, therefore suggesting that her intentions to marry Anjou were false, this argument ultimately overlooks her true character and ignores the detail between the lines of her letters to the duke and her works of poetry. The modern iconography of Elizabeth has become as much of a cult as it was during her own lifetime, and though she half-invented, half-inherited the courtly cult of love that now identifies her unique reign, this narrative has distorted the reality behind a courtship perhaps far more interesting than that of her parents. We commonly refer to Elizabeth as the 'Mistress of England', the virgin queen who vowed herself into a life of chastity and perpetual virginity. She even used her unique role as a female monarch to convince the men around her that she was already married – to the Kingdom of England. This was how she chose to rule, allowing for her courtiers to shower her with attention, as a Tudor courtier would have showered attention upon his betrothed. Here, she flipped her perceived weakness in virginity to that of an iconic, all-powerful female monarch, who sacrificed her own 'natural purpose' and personal happiness for the sake of her people.[1]

This image of Elizabeth was of her own design, and though it wasn't uncommon for Tudor monarchs to alter their image for propaganda purposes, historians are usually quick to call out any inaccuracies based on how each monarch wished to be portrayed. Yet, the image Elizabeth created is widely accepted and goes unquestioned, her true feelings and desires masked by the public necessity for national identity. It may be true that she lived and died a virgin, and we know that she never married nor had any children despite the rumours – if she had, history may well have been very different. However, this does not mean that she was incapable of the natural human desire for intimacy and close relationships. It has been argued that her close and personal relationship to Lord Robert Dudley became sexual. So why is it that many scholars and the public alike refuse to view her in a different light? The evidence is available, yet there exists a fear of altering her story to suit a more realistic and nuanced narrative because to do so would somewhat alter her image as the iconic Gloriana. Recently, a scholarly discourse regarding the political, social, and cultural implementations of the queen's iconic virginity has come about. This has allowed for some reconsiderations regarding her relationships with her male courtiers and suitors, and although it has been argued by others that she and Anjou had affection for one another, even loved each other, the available narrative of this courtship continues to be dismissed.

To many, Elizabeth is Gloriana, while, to some, she is Pandora – a complete paradox – then, to others, she is Cynthia, Eliza, or Astraea. These different names that have been attached to her since the beginning of her reign right up to today are symbolic of how she wished to be viewed herself, how her courtiers or sixteenth-century poets and playwrights wished to portray her, and how we, in hindsight, wish to identify with her. However, the truth behind Elizabeth is rather more complex, yet underwhelming, in comparison to that of the 'mythical maiden'. In many ways, the modern image of her, which does not consider her relationship with Anjou to be anything but political, is strikingly similar to that of how she actually looked as an aging woman, in contrast to how she wished to be seen. It is likely that she would have wished us to view her the way we do today, and she would probably not enjoy the interpretations of her letters to the duke, which reveal her true feelings. Yet, it is not the job of the historian, nor the duty of the reader to adhere to these probable wishes. To gain a better understanding of the social and cultural importance of her image, we have to strip her down to the bare minimum of her own mortality and humanity.

How she is viewed as an important historical figure, expressed through both academic and popular interpretations, is often far from reality. In our desire to identify with Elizabeth the queen, we forget that she was a real woman, with real feelings, desires, worries, and ailments. When thinking about her as the ageing queen, it is easy to imagine the inch-thick make-up, rich red wigs, and elegant clothing and jewelry, when underneath this iconic image of 'Gloriana' was a rather lonely, old woman, seemingly full of regrets, according to her poetry. After Anjou died, she became very different to the young, vivacious queen she had once been. In essence, the queen began to fade, as would her memories and true feelings. For many years after her death, her feelings about Anjou were left unknown. The courtiers who once honoured her, worshipped her, even, would soon have another sovereign to honour, or were replaced entirely.

There is no doubt that the iconology that exists today regarding Elizabeth's love life and the tragedy surrounding it, began with theatrical portrayals. Yet, most popular or theatrical interpretations of her love life concentrate on her relationship with Robert Dudley, her 'sweet Robin'. Though it might be true that she loved him in her youth, and greatly mourned his death, though with somewhat less pomp and ceremony than Anjou's, there is no doubt that when she embarked on her last courtship, any romantic love she held for Dudley was gone, replaced by a close friendship, which she evidently needed.

The cult that had grown around her image is a testimony to her character, strength, resilience, and effectiveness as a ruler, and yet, she was often insecure in all of these traits we so easily attribute to her today. Like she did during her reign, we dress her as we would like to see her, a symbol of purity, virtue, and strength, along with her wholesome Englishness. However, we must remember that the virgin queen may have felt different inwardly, and if she were not to have inherited her sister's crown, she may well have married and had children. As a princess of ancient royal blood, with connections to some of the greatest royal houses in Europe, it would not be surprising that she may have married if she had not been queen. This is where Elizabeth remains a paradox, for her main duty as the monarch was to marry and produce an heir. It was her precarious position as a Protestant queen, and perhaps her traumatic past, that would ultimately make it impossible for her to marry and bear children. When considering gender normativity regarding marriage and pregnancy in Tudor England, Elizabeth clearly went against the grain, though probably not due to her own desires.

By the time she was in her sixties, most noblewomen around her, especially her kin, were surrounded by their children and ever-growing families, including grandchildren and great-grandchildren. In this, Elizabeth's female contemporaries had much more comfort and wealth than that of a queen. They had a supportive and loving family, something that she, divine as she seemed, could no longer have or even demand. Her symbolic virginity went even further than this, setting her apart in relativity to those around her who had lived very real lives. Though her life and reign were dramatic and often chaotic, it was far from normal. Her iconic image, projected by how she presented herself, also set her apart in terms of mortality; she seemed eternal. Yet, the ageing queen was far from exempt in this regard, and though her looks and even charms began to fade, she would have clung to any reminder of her youth and, most likely, her great loves. She had never known what it was to be a wife, despite her efforts in pretence during Anjou's final visit to England, nor would she ever become a mother, something she seemingly struggled with during her later years, yet entirely ignored during her youth. It would seem that she, too, was blinded by her own glory for a time.[2]

The public opposition to Elizabeth and Anjou's intention to marry was later supported by the growing iconography of the virgin queen. Though the reasons for creating an iconic, goddess-like representation of female monarchy were mainly founded in opposition to perhaps her true love, as it further developed over the centuries, the real Elizabeth, the woman behind the mask of monarchy, faded and has become lost to us. Yet, this was not without her own encouragement, and it is likely that the latter years of her reign depended on her immortal image. As queen, she stated that she was married to her kingdom, even mentioned that she was wife or mother to her subjects. Speaking of her people in 1599, she referred to them as 'all my husbands, my good people'.[3] This was a clever tactic she used later in her life to preserve her legacy, rather than to resist marriage.

By 1584, it was clear that she would never marry, nor could expect a suitor to come courting. It is simply no longer good enough to say that 'we do not know enough about Elizabeth's true feelings for Anjou', when the evidence, often in her own hand and in the reports of others, states otherwise. What historians choose to interpret and how they interpret it will always be based on some form of bias. In relation to Elizabeth and Anjou, this bias has been handed down through the centuries, preserving an even thicker mask than the queen herself could have imagined. The modern image of her isn't simply there because we want it to be – it exists because it suits a narrative that not only draws an audience, it suits the shared conception of national identity. However, the society in which Elizabeth lived is long gone, and though it is the duty of the historian to interpret the many elements of that time, the overall understanding of the Tudor period, and Elizabeth's reign, has been distorted to suit modern ideals and notions of morality and nation states. During Elizabeth's time, this was not so dissimilar.

Her society still worshipped the Virgin Mary, an image that held precedence in courtly love since the early medieval period. The connection between Elizabeth's image and the image of the Holy Virgin was therefore easily applied, and even necessary, especially in her defiance of the Spanish Armada. She would become dependent on this image later on in her reign, and it was probably due to her own vanity as much as it was to do with political iconography and legacy. While she cultivated the courtly cult of love that marked her early reign, she would also cultivate an image so powerful that it leans towards idolatry.[4]

The death of Anjou was a hard blow to take. Her public mourning, letters and poetry, make the likelihood of her true love for him, and possibly his for her, almost certain. Yet, she would continue to have favourites, even into her old age. In the years following Anjou's death, she found comfort in surrounding herself with younger, handsome courtiers. However, one thing is apparent – though she may have enjoyed the flattery of these young courtiers, the intense years of romance and courtship had long gone, and it could even be said that this part of her went with Anjou.[5] She had played the marriage game for many years, had loved and lost, and came seriously close to marrying a man she really loved, or at least had great affection for. During this time, she had triumphed over the might of Spain, crushed Philip's fleet, and proved England to be a powerful and rich kingdom. Indeed, her reign is often referred to as England's 'Golden Age'.

Some of her favourites had been present throughout her courtship with Anjou, and though her relationship with Dudley and his reaction to her display of love for the duke is often a topic of discussion, little else is offered to the reader of how her other favourites reacted to her change in mind to marry. As we know, she liked to give her favourites names. Dudley was her 'eyes', and Anjou was her 'frog', yet there were many male courtiers with nicknames during the 1570s and 1580s, and even long after Anjou's death. If Dudley was her eyes, then the courtier

Sir Christopher Hatton, who was said to be both handsome and charming, was 'Lids'. Though close in nickname to that of Dudley, it is likely that Hatton's pet name was due to the symbols represented in their letters that resemble eyes. It seems that his affection for the queen was based on an infatuation, which went much further than that of the cult of love she had created around her and encouraged. Hatton believed himself to be in love with the queen, and as a result of this love, and because of her vow to never marry, he, too, remained unmarried, confessing that he was overcome by his passion for her:

> I will wash away the faults of these letters with the drops from your poor Lids, and so enclose them. Would God I were with you but for one hour. My wits are overwrought with thoughts. I find myself amazed. Bear with me, my most dearest sweet Lady, Passion overcometh me. I can write no more. Love me; for I love you.[6]

Hatton's forwardness in his expression of love was not entirely unique during Elizabeth's reign but his reaction to her courtship with Anjou, which resembles that of Dudley's, is much more telling. When Dudley was disgraced for a time due to his secret marriage to Lettice Knollys, Hatton became Elizabeth's favourite go-to courtier for a time. That was until negotiations of marriage between she and Anjou began. When she publicly announced her intentions to marry him during his second visit to England, it is said that Hatton burst into tears. However, though he would grow wealthier and his position rose so high that he was appointed Lord Chancellor in 1587, Elizabeth's affection for him often depended on her mood, with her favouritism for him fluctuating. Reportedly, and rather humorously, her indecisiveness regarding her liking of Hatton left him in a perpetual state of anxiety and anguished worship.[7] Perhaps his over-eagerness made her so unsure of him. Some state that it was because of the rise of Sir Walter Raleigh in her favour, yet he would also suffer greatly as the queen's favourite, ending up in the Tower on at least one occasion.

It is far more likely that the loss and death of Anjou had such a profound effect on Elizabeth, that the cult she had developed around her was no longer enough to fill the void of loneliness that came with being the 'Virgin Queen'. For all its necessity, the iconography of Elizabeth was as much of a curse to her personal life as it was a necessity to her political and cultural role. Hatton's state of anxiety due to her fluctuating favour for him is evident in a letter he wrote to her in 1580, where he states: 'I should sin, most gracious sovereign, against a Holy Ghost, most damnably, if towards Your Highness I should be found unthankful.'[8]

The language here is recognizable as that typically used by Elizabeth's male courtiers in reference to her status as the 'Virgin Queen', a living, breathing religious symbol of purity and chasteness they could offer devotion to. This was the queen's own creation, yet, for all of Hatton's efforts, his devotion never earned him the recognition and place in her favour he desired. It seems that Raleigh's elevation certainly came about around the same time as Anjou's departure and the ending of the Anglo-French negotiations of marriage. If Hatton thought this moment as his chance to rise in favour, he would be greatly disappointed. What he had to offer Elizabeth as a favourite was dull in comparison to that of Raleigh, who offered his queen adventure and lavish gifts. Not only this but Raleigh was extremely good-looking, even by modern standards if his portrait is in any way a true representation of the man, and he shared Elizabeth's love of flashy, showy clothing, which no doubt made him seem a shining star compared to Hatton.[9]

Raleigh was different to Hatton, coming from humbler origins, and though he was a true adventurer, he was also a more honest, down-to-earth countryman, who most likely fascinated the queen due to their common sense of wit, humour, and intellectual abilities. Yet, his creativity and artistic ability as a man of the country would also have intrigued her, because while she was by this time fading in terms of her own physical beauty, she had an increased curiosity for knowledge. It is well known that she kept up her studies of foreign languages and cultures, astronomy, and was a gifted composer and artist. Raleigh was also a gifted poet, something we now know Elizabeth would have found irresistible. Being a friend of contemporary poets, such as Spenser and Marlowe, would have allowed him to use this as a way of pushing himself towards the queen's highest favour. He set to wooing her with poetry, which appealed to her vanity and need to portray herself as the 'immortal' goddess, and he even referred to her as the 'Moon Goddess' in a poem, ultimately dismissing the fact that she was by this time in her fifties – considerably old by Tudor standards, even for a queen. By recognizing her as a demi-goddess, and a beautiful woman, Raleigh fed her needs as his sovereign and as a woman. The language in his poetry is rather romantic, convincing the reader of his devotion to his queen:

Time wears her not, she doth his chariot guide,
Mortality below her orb is placed…
In her is Virtue's Perfect image cast.
…That wit, which of my thoughts doth hold the reins.[10]

Elizabeth enjoyed her flirtations with him, and even gave him the nickname 'Water', which was probably to make fun of his Christian name 'Walter'. This is because the pronunciation for both 'Walter' and 'water' was almost identical in the late-sixteenth century. Hatton, disturbed by his queen's favouritism for Raleigh, is said to have sent her a golden bucket as a gesture of this overt jealousy. Though Raleigh, Hatton, Essex, and many others would attempt to woo Elizabeth for her favour, she would never view this courtly cult of love and worship quite the same way after the departure and death of her dear frog. She was quite willing to have favourites and lap up their attention, poetry, and gifts but they could never give her what she had with Anjou – a chance at true love, marriage, and happiness. It is probable that she favoured men such as Raleigh out of necessity – borne of loneliness.

Though she began to surround herself with younger and newer men, with fresher ideas, it was something she loathed because many of the men who had been with her from her youth had either betrayed her, retired, or died. Many blows other than that of the death of Anjou would come during the latter twenty years of her reign, and this only added to her often-reported melancholic state. After her defeat of the Spanish Armada, she was portrayed as 'God's chosen one', thus, Gloriana. This only added to the already existing and growing iconography of Elizabeth during her reign, and would continue into the seventeenth century, before taking hold again during the nineteenth century, giving us the image we have today of her. Yet, despite all her victories, she found defeat in the deaths of her many favourites, especially Dudley and Burghley.

Though Dudley had betrayed his queen and was no longer her most favourite man at court, he had stuck by her as closely as he could, and his dedication to her in his later years cannot be denied. Amidst the celebration of the victory over Spain's Armada in the autumn of 1588, Elizabeth lost her 'sweet Robin' to the clutches of death while he was travelling to the Baths of Buxton in an attempt to revive himself and treat his many ailments. It seems that he had been unwell for some time, and his loss is said to have devastated her. They had recently put their differences behind them and she seemed much happier and perkier than she had in a long time, possibly since the death of Anjou. On hearing of Dudley's demise, she displayed the same dramatics as when reports of Anjou's death reached her. Yet, this seemed slightly more extreme. She locked herself in her chamber for several days, refusing to eat and sleep until, eventually, her council were forced to have the doors broken down and persuaded her (with great difficulty) to return to her court and duties as queen.[11]

Her reaction to Dudley's death has often been used by historians to suit the narrative that she had always been in love with him. Yet, though it is true that she held a special place for him, she also reacted dramatically when many of her favourites died. Perhaps the overwhelming feeling of age and the loneliness that accompanied it brought on such dramatic displays of mourning. Yet, her grief cannot be denied, either, as she had been close to Dudley since she was a child. Many more deaths were to follow Anjou and Dudley's, and the days to come would fill the virgin queen with sorrow and regret. Even so, her fascination with handsome and intelligent men would never cease, and this is a testimony to the resilience of her character. The death of Blanche Parry, her Chief Gentlewoman of the Privy Chamber, would also have a profound effect on the ageing monarch. Blanch had served the queen since she was a young girl, and perhaps knew her more than any other female attendant since Kat Ashely.[12]

The death of Hatton would also send her into the depths of despair, regardless of her fluctuating fondness for him. Despite her overt uncertainty towards him, Hatton had remained a faithful and loyal subject, his love for her unquestionable. He would fund or invest in expeditions to the New World, of which some were ironically led by Sir Walter Raleigh. Raleigh would also bring tragedy himself, though not by means of death. It was revealed to the ageing queen that he, her undisputed favourite, had been involved in a sexual affair, and had even married Elizabeth Throckmorton, one of her favoured Maids of Honour. This had been going on for some time and right under her nose. Throckmorton was also pregnant by the time the couple secretly married and this would have had a profound effect on Elizabeth's state of mind, considering her losses in Dudley and Anjou. She was also aware that, as everyone around her was fading or dying, she would be left with nobody to share the memories of her youth with. The fact that she was childless and had no named heir would have also had an impact on her reaction to Throckmorton and Raleigh's betrayal. It would also have echoed the memory of Dudley's betrayal in marrying Lettice Knollys in the 1570s. She would send the couple to the Tower, yet would soon relent and allow them their freedom and to remain married. Though she would later fund Raleigh's venture to New Guiana, she never fully trusted him again, and Elizabeth Throckmorton, or 'Bess' as she was nicknamed, never fully returned to favour.[13] Interestingly, Walter was released from the Tower before Bess.

Elizabeth's court had always been full of temptations, for the queen herself as much as the courtiers who filled it. Yet, she found pride in her perpetual virginity and wanted her court to reflect that symbol of chastity and duty. In reality, her courtiers were more promiscuous and flirtatious than was expected and this led to many couples being exiled or imprisoned for marrying without royal permission. This was probably not so much due to her own personal losses in love as it was about her wishes to portray herself as 'Gloriana', England's virgin queen. If she were to keep this image of purity during her own lifetime, a strict maintenance of an ethical tone and moral standing was necessary and her courtiers would not have been ignorant to this. But, as is typical with human nature, love and lust would often get in the way of this construction of purity. She almost succumbed to it herself on a number of occasions with Dudley and Anjou, at least, as is evident in her letters and other writings.

However, duty would always prevail, and when the one person who constantly reminded the queen of that duty died, she would never be the same, and it could be said that the death of William Cecil brought on the sunset of Gloriana's reign. William Cecil – Lord Burghley – the queen's 'eyes', died on 4th August 1598, at the grand age of seventy-eight – ancient by

Tudor standards. He had served his queen so well and was so favoured by her that it is said she fed him soup with her own hand during his last days.[14] This was the final blow for Elizabeth, as she had relied on Burghley for most of her reign. Though he was replaced by his son, Robert Cecil, she could never trust him the way she did his father. She would go on to live another five years after the death of Burghley. Robert Cecil, or 'Pygmy' as she called him, would inherit a monumental task and ran most state business during the queen's latter years. The reliance on new, younger men at court may well have kept her going for some time but it may have ultimately reminded her of the fragility of her legacy and the Tudor dynasty. It would also have brought into focus a past that could not be altered, with no more 'second chances' to come.

Robert Devereux, the Earl of Essex, would also grow high in favour but would ultimately attempt to undermine her rule and try to take power for himself in 1601. Elizabeth had no choice but to sign the death warrant for her sweet Robin's stepson, and Lettice Knollys' eldest son. This irony may not have been so sweet for the ageing queen but her safety and security became paramount over that of courtly favouritism.

The execution of Essex was widely unpopular amongst the public, and Elizabeth would never quite recover from it. He was greatly favoured by the ageing queen due to his close hereditary ties to her through his mother's and her own family. Though his mother would never return to Elizabeth's favour, Essex may have reminded her of her once close confidant and perhaps first-love, Robert Dudley, who, upon marrying Knollys, became Essex's stepfather. Essex soon became known as a public hero as well as a traitor, thanks to Shakespeare. However, the anger was not directed at the queen but at Burghley's son and successor, Robert. He was depicted as a 'devil' prior to Essex's execution and his position would only allow the public's hatred for him to grow. Perhaps, as Leanda de Lisle points out, people hoped that after Essex's traitor's death, the queen would remember why he complained in the first place, but they would be disappointed. As one hero's martyrdom was becoming more and more popular, Elizabeth began to fade. The queen had clearly aged beyond recognition, and the following months after Essex's execution would put her under enormous strain, thus causing her mental and physical health to deteriorate. By November 1601, when she was to open her final parliament, she is said to have almost been crushed under the weight of her ceremonial robes.

She was right to worry about her people's opinions, as Cecil had raised the price of starch, which outraged the public. Though the queen was fading, she was clearly still capable of taking on the concerns of her subjects. It would not be her ageing figure or inability to walk in her own ceremonial robes that her people would remember with pride but her 'golden speech' of 30th November. This may well have been the queen's final farewell to her subjects as a whole and, ever the pragmatist, she took the opportunity to inform them of the pressures she had endured due to her position. This was her final piece of theatre, and she knew it. She stated that 'To be a king and wear a crown is a thing more glorious to them that see it than it is pleasant to them that bear it'. Though this may be the queen referring to the pressures brought on by the crown, it may also be a direct reference to the fact that she chose duty over her own pleasure. It seems that the burden of monarchy had not only saved Elizabeth and England from the wrath of her sister's reign, and given her a life of luxury and splendour, it also limited her abilities in many ways and put a true adventurer at heart in a cage. The crown and the almighty weight it brought also blocked her from marrying the man she wanted, whether that be interpreted as Dudley or Anjou. Elizabeth the woman was replaced by Elizabeth Regina, Gloriana – the Virgin Queen.

The queen, however, was clever to remind her people that, in many ways, she was simply the means by which God could comfort and care for the people of England, and she declared this in her last speech:

> For myself, I was never so much enticed with the glorious name of a king of royal authority of a queen as delighted that God hath made me His instrument to maintain His truth and glory, and to defend this kingdom from peril, dishonour, tyranny and oppression.[15]

Clearly, Elizabeth was still capable of forming her image as she would like to have been seen. Perhaps she knew she was approaching the end of her life, and was concerned with the preservation of her image. It is also likely that she wished to express to her people that though she was in many ways happy to have reigned over them, the personal cost of the crown was one that brought emotional bankruptcy. She also refers to her people lovingly in this speech, a reminder that her love of them was greater than any love she bore for a man:

> For it is not my desire to live nor reign, longer than my life and reign shall be for your good. And though you have had and may have many princes more mighty and wise sitting in this seat, yet you never had or shall have any that will be more careful and loving.[16]

The inherited version of Elizabeth I that we recognize today may well be the image the queen herself would have liked us to see. She may well have worked for most of the end of her reign after the death of Anjou to secure this image of a pious, chaste, and goddess-like figure whose legacy would rule over England for eternity. Yet, as history as a discipline has developed over the past century, allowing us to root out the true character behind some of the past's most famous figures, some no longer wish to see the glorified, stainless images of our predecessors because, in today's social climate, they are no longer relatable. However, Elizabeth's image, whether it be of Gloriana, the Virgin Queen, the downcast, bastardized princess, or the queen with many secret lovers, continues to attract the attention of millions of people. The representation of her as how she wished to be seen resonates more with her 'fans' today than that of Elizabeth the woman, who loved, lost, and had to fight tactically to gain what she desired and to stay in power. It should be the latter version of Elizabeth, the true woman, we should look for. Her final days are revealing of the more human side to this queen who has captured the hearts of many.

By early 1603, she had survived almost every obstacle that could have been placed in her path. She remained unmarried and childless, yet was loved beyond measure by her people. Throughout her reign, she had played the game of love but lost. She created a cult of courtly love that her father would envy, and she had executed her power in a way that could only have made her mother proud. Her intelligence was incomparable, her wit unmatchable, her rage often uncontrollable, and her diligence and skillfulness as a ruler unprecedented. She survived the disgrace of her mother's execution, and the psychological consequences of her stepfather's molestation. Later, she encountered love and lost it on more than one occasion. She wished to marry and have children but she also feared it. It is accepted that she loved her cousin and fellow queen, Mary Stuart, as a sister, but she would also have to sign her death warrant. Elizabeth had lived, loved, and lost in numerous ways. She chose to inhabit her sovereignty alone, at great personal cost, and without a king to rule beside her. In many ways, she became king herself, defying gender normativity. By the following spring, she had reached her seventieth year and the forty-fifth of her reign. It seemed like she may go on forever. But even kings are made of flesh.

She became more fatigued, racked with insomnia, and her memory began to fail her. Along with this, she suffered from loss of eyesight and complained of pains in her arm and side – probably arthritis and gout, and her old foe, melancholy, now referred to as depression, would make an appearance on more than one occasion. Her decline in health was swift, as only the previous year, though tired, she seemed to be in robust health, with little complaint other than what was typical of a woman of her age.[17] It was decided that the court should move to Richmond Palace from Whitehall that spring but, by March, everyone could see that the queen was deteriorating. Her insomnia was worse than ever before, and her appetite had all but vanished, which was unusual for her, having grown rather plump in her old age. By mid-March, her physician diagnosed inflammation of the breast and throat. Cecil thus activated his plans for the succession of James VI of England, which he had been secretly organizing for some time. Contrary to popular belief, for all of Cecil's organizational skills, James' succession would be far from smooth.[18]

Elizabeth became so weak that she could no longer attend prayer but nor would she take to her bed. Instead, she sat or lay on cushions on her floor, provided for by her many ladies. She would not be left alone for a single moment, probably afraid that if she went to bed, she would never get back out of it. And she was right. She refused to change her clothes or wash, and had not seen her reflection in some time. Rather than allow their mistress to suffer her image, her ladies had smashed all looking glasses. Elizabeth clearly suffered from health issues, both mental and physical, towards the end of her life that may well be treatable today. The Earl of Nottingham attempted to encourage his queen to go to bed, without avail, as she quickly replied, 'If you were in the habit of seeing such things in your bed as I see in mine, you would not persuade me to go there'.[19] This must be in reference to her insomnia and nightmares. She suffered greatly from these troubles in the final days of Anjou's last visit to England. During this time, she was well aware that she would have to call off the courtship for religious and political reasons but the guilt and the betrayal of her own heart would have influenced her inner turmoil. Was her mental state during her final days a reflection of the loss of Anjou, Dudley, or even Burghley? Or was it the loneliness that came with her age that would ultimately kill her? There are many theories as to what killed the Virgin Queen. Some say breast cancer, some say blood poisoning from her lead-based make-up, which is the most ironic yet plausible theory. Others say it was a bronchial infection, pneumonia, or a weakened immune system, while some theorize that she simply died of old age. It is hard to pinpoint the direct cause of her death due to the lack of post-mortem. However, considering all these ailments, one factor has often been ignored: her loneliness.

Throughout her reign, Elizabeth became iconic, goddess-like, yet she was not immortal. Nor were her contemporaries. Though she lived a considerably long life, this meant that when the end was nigh, she was surrounded by people who had not witnessed the beginning of her reign, the struggle to secure the safety of her own life, and the plight of negotiating many suitors from home and abroad. She spent much of her early reign avoiding marriage but not love, yet when she finally found a fitting suitor who would bring her stability, companionship, and even love, it was denied her – not just by her council or subjects but by herself. The virgin queen was capable of feeling love and heartbreak but was also notably susceptible to loneliness. Though the way in which we remember her would flatter her vanity, it is this vanity that undermines her truth, as do her portraits. The virgin queen may have died surrounded by people who professed to love her, and who she professed to love, but her final hours indicate the loneliness felt by this iconic woman. There were no children or grandchildren weeping at her bedside, and no husband to mourn the setting sun that had once shone so brightly.

She was eventually persuaded to take to her bed. Elizabeth I died on 24th March 1603, haunted by the many ghosts of her past. Without a single word or sound, she slipped into a deep sleep and never woke up. What was she thinking in her final moments? Who did she wish to see the most? Was it the face of her humble advisor, Burghley? Was it her mother and father? Was it her first love, Robert Dudley? Or was it the only man she had hoped to spend these final moments of her life with, the Duke of Anjou – her Frog Prince? We will never know but that will never stop us searching for answers, trying to see behind the image of Elizabeth handed to us by history.

Notes

Chapter 1 - A Courtly Cult of Love

1. John Guy, *Elizabeth: the forgotten years*, (London, 2016), pp. 11-12.
2. Ibid.
3. David Loades, *Mary Tudor: a life*, (Oxford, 1989), pp. 199-201.
4. J. Aylmer, *An harborowe for faithful and trewe subiects*, (London, 1559), Fordham University online. https://sourcebooks.fordham.edu/mod/1559Alymer-haborowe.asp asp (29 Apr. 2020). Also see Guy, *Elizabeth*, p. 11.
5. Ibid.
6. Lisa Hilton, *Elizabeth: renaissance prince, a biography*, (London, 2014), pp. 33-34.
7. Ibid.
8. Tracy Borman, *The private lives of the Tudors: uncovering the secrets of Britain's greatest dynasty*, (London, 2016), p. 271. Also see Christopher Hibbert, *Elizabeth I: a personal history of the virgin queen*, (London, 1992), p. 67.
9. Borman, *The private lives*, p. 272.
10. Elizabeth I, Hatfield, 20 Nov. 1558 (NA, SP12/1 fol. 12), National Archives online, https://www.nationalarchives.gov.uk/education/resources/elizabeth-monarchy/elizabeths-first-speech/, (3 May 2020).
11. Leanda de Lisle, *Tudor; the family story*, (London, 2013), p. 354. Also see Steven W. May (ed.), *Queen Elizabeth I: selected works*, (New York, 2004), p. 12.
12. De Lisle, *Tudor*, pp. 354-355.
13. Norman Jones, *The birth of the Elizabethan age: England in the 1560s*, (Cambridge, 1993), p. 119.
14. Bruce Heydt, 'Amy Robsart's revenge?' in *British Heritage*, vol. 25, iss. 1 (2004), pp. 28-33.
15. David Loades, *Elizabeth I*, (London, 2003), p. 139.

16. Ibid.
17. Guy, *Elizabeth*, p. 45. Also see *Calendar of state papers, foreign, general series, Elizabeth I, letters and papers, June-July 1559* (NA Kew, SP 70/5, fos. 183-184).
18. Coroner's report into the death of Amy Robsart, Aug. 1561 (NA, King's bench records, 9/1073, fol. 80), National Archives online, https://www.nationalarchives.gov.uk/education/resources/elizabeth-monarchy/coroners-report/, (7 May 2020).
19. Guy, *Elizabeth*, p. 45.
20. Simon Adams, G.W. Bernard (eds.), *Religion, politics, and society in sixteenth-century England*, (Cambridge, 2003), p. 66.
21. Guy, *Elizabeth*, p. 45.
22. William Camden, *The history of the most renowned and victorious princess Elizabeth, late queen of England*, ed. Wallace T. MacCaffrey, (Chicago, 1970), p. 29.
23. T.E Hartley, *Proceedings in the parliaments of Elizabeth I, vol. 1* (Leicester, 1981), p. 45. Note: the 'marble' is a reference to her tomb.
24. Alison Weir, *The life of Elizabeth*, (New York, 1998), p. 51.
25. Borman, *The private lives*, p. 315.
26. Ibid.
27. Anne Somerset, *Ladies in waiting: from the Tudors to the present day*, (London, 2005), p. 61.
28. Nicola Tallis, *Elizabeth's rival: the tumultuous tale of Lettice Knollys, countess of Leicester*, (London, 2017), *Dramatis Personae xix*.
29. W. Murdin (ed.) *A collection of state papers relating to affairs in the reign of queen Elizabeth from the year 1571 to 1576*, (London, 1759), p. 301. Also see Tallis, *Elizabeth's rival*, p. 146.
30. Tallis, *Elizabeth's rival*, p. 147.
31. Tallis, *Elizabeth's rival*, p. 166.
32. Tallis, *Elizabeth's rival*, p. 171.
33. Tallis, *Elizabeth's rival*, p. 167.

34. Tallis, *Elizabeth's rival*, p. 174.
35. William Camden, *The history of the most renowned and victorious princess Elizabeth, late queen of England*, (London, 1688), pp. 232-233, Google Books online, https://play.google.com/books/reader?id=PV6t0sYd4a8C&pg=GBS.PP11, (10 May 2020).
36. Ibid.
37. Tallis, *Elizabeth's rival*, pp. 180-181.

Chapter 2 - The Pursuit of a Queen

1. John N. King, 'Queen Elizabeth I: representations of the virgin queen' in *Renaissance Quarterly*, vol. 43, no. 1, (1990), pp 30-74 at p. 39.
2. Roy Strong, *Gloriana: the portraits of queen Elizabeth I*, (London, 1987), pp. 22-25.
3. E.P. Cheyney, review of 'King, queen, Jack: Philip of Spain courts Elizabeth' by Milton Waldman in *The Journal of Modern History*, vol. 4, no. 1, (1932), pp. 115-116.
4. Ibid.
5. Susan Doran, *Monarchy and matrimony: the courtships of Elizabeth I*, (London, 1996), pp. 37-38.
6. Doran, *Monarchy and matrimony*, p. 44.
7. Anna Whitelock, *Mary Tudor: England's first queen,* (London, 2009), pp. 222-223.
8. Doran, *Monarchy and matrimony*, p. 41.
9. The Lady Elizabeth to Sir Thomas Pope, 26 Apr. 1558 (BL Harleian MS 444, fols. 20-29).
10. Elizabeth I to King Eric XIV of Sweden, 25 Feb. 1560 (NA, SP 70/11 f. 74), National Archives online, https://www.nationalarchives.gov.uk/education/resources/elizabeth-monarchy/elizabeth-i-to-king-eric-xiv-of-sweden/ (12 May 2020).
11. Lloyd E. Berry (ed.), *John Stubbs's 'Gaping Gulf' with letters and other relevant documents*, (Charlottesville, 1968), p. 49.

12. Borman, *The private lives*, p. 281.
13. Hilton, *Elizabeth*, p. 149.
14. Ibid.
15. Carole Levin, *The heart and stomach of a king: Elizabeth I and the politics of sex and power*, (Philadelphia, 2013), p. 42.
16. Levin, *The heart and stomach of a king*, p. 43.
17. King, 'Queen Elizabeth I', p. 39.
18. Levin, *The heart and stomach of a king*, p. 45. Also see Philip Yorke Hardwicke (ed.), *Miscellaneous state papers: from 1501 to 1726, vol. 1*, (London, 1778), p. 174, Google books online, https://books.google.ie/books?id=L34gAQAAMAAJ&printsec=frontcover&source=gbs_ge_summary_r&cad=0#v=onepage&q&f=false (13 May 2020).
19. de Lisle, *Tudor*, p. 357.
20. Penry Williams, *The later Tudors: England 1547-1603*, (Oxford, 1995), p. 229.
21. Josephine Ross, *The men who would be king: the courtships of queen Elizabeth I*, (New York, 2011), p. 59.
22. de Lisle, *Tudor*, p. 357.
23. Ross, *The men who would be king*, p. 149.
24. Levin, *The heart and stomach of a king*, pp. 40-65.
25. Guy, *Elizabeth*, p. 46.
26. Guy, *Elizabeth*, p. 47.
27. Ibid.
28. Linda Porter, *Katherine the queen, the remarkable life of Katherine Parr*, (London, 2010), pp 309-310.
29. Guy, *Elizabeth*, p. 47.
30. Porter, *Katherine the queen*, p. 37.
31. Paul E. J. Hammer, 'Sex and the virgin queen: aristocratic concupiscence and the court of Elizabeth I' in *The Sixteenth Century Journal*, vol. 31, no. 1, (2000), pp 77-97 at pp 80-81.
32. Ibid.
33. Doran, *Monarchy and matrimony*, p. 69.
34. Natalie Mears, 'Love-making and diplomacy: Elizabeth I and

the Anjou marriage negotiations, c.1578-1582' in *History*, vol. 86, no. 284, (2001), pp. 442-466.

35. Doran, *Monarchy and matrimony*, p. 69.
36. Ibid.

Chapter 3 - From Alençon to Anjou

1. Mears, 'Love-making and diplomacy' p. 443.
2. Guy, *Elizabeth*, p. 47.
3. Leah S. Marcus, Janel M. Mueller, and Mary Beth Rose, *Elizabeth I: collected works*, (Chicago, 2000), p. 233.
4. Aryn Elizabeth Bell, 'Elizabeth I and the policy of marriage: the Anjou match, 1572-1582', M.A thesis, University of North Dakoda, (North Dakota, 2013), p. 47.
5. Mack P. Holt, *The duke of Anjou and the politique struggle during the wars of religion*, (Cambridge, 1986), pp. 2-4.
6. Holt, *The duke of Anjou*, p. 242.
7. Holt, *The duke of Anjou*, p. 10.
8. Peter Ackroyd, *Tudors: the history of England*, (London, 2012), p. 386.
9. Levin, *The heart and stomach of a king*, p. 55.
10. Mack P. Holt, 'Patterns of clientèle and economic opportunity at court during the wars of religion: the household of François, Duke of Anjou' in *French Historical Studies*, vol. 13, no. 3 (1984), pp 305-322 at p. 308.
11. Ibid.
12. Dorothy Thickett, *Etienne Pasquier: lettres historiques pour les années 1556-1594*, (Geneva, 1966), pp. 441-442.
13. Holt, 'Patterns of clientèle' p. 308.
14. Robert J. Knecht, *The French religious wars 1562-98*, (Harlow, 2000), pp. 53-54.
15. Hilton, *Elizabeth*, p. 228.
16. Hilton, *Elizabeth*, p. 239.
17. Holt, 'Patterns of clientèle' p. 314.
18. Carlo M. Bajetta, Guillaume Coatalen, and Jonathan Gibson

(eds.), *Elizabeth I's correspondence: letters, rhetoric and politics*, (New York, 2014), pp 34-35. This wonderful book includes the original contents of Elizabeth's six holograph letters in French to Anjou, with added transcription and text analysis.

19. Portrait of Prince Hercule François, Duc d'Alençon 1572, (NGAW), National Gallery of Art, Washington online, https://www.wga.hu/html_m/m/master/yunk_fr/yunk_fr1/124princ.html, (22 May 2020). Note: there exists little to go on in terms of analysis of this portrait of Anjou, considering the artist is unknown. Its likeness to his appearance is therefore subjective.

20/ Bajetta, Coatalen, and Gibson, *Elizabeth I's correspondence*, p. 32.

Chapter 4 - The Language of Love

1. Doran, *Monarchy and matrimony*, p. 216.

2. Hilton, *Elizabeth*, p. 34.

3. Borman, *The private lives*, p. 337.

4. Bajetta, Coatalen, and Gibson, *Elizabeth I's correspondence*, pp. 34-35.

5. Introduction in *Calendar of the Cecil papers in Hatfield House, vol. 2, 1572-1582*, (London, 1888), pp iii-1, British History online, https://www.british-history.ac.uk/cal-cecil-papers/vol2/iii-l, (17 July 2021).

6. The Duke of Anjou to the queen, 2 Mar. 1579, *Calendar of the Cecil papers..., vol. 2*, (London, 1888), pp 234-245, British History online, https://www.british-history.ac.uk/cal-cecil-papers/vol2/pp234-245 (17 Jul. 2021).

7. The Duke of Anjou to the queen, 8 Mar. 1579, *Calendar of the Cecil papers..., vol. 2*, (London, 1888), pp 234-245, British History online, https://www.british-history.ac.uk/cal-cecil-papers/vol2/pp234-245 (17 Jul. 2021).

8. Bajetta, Coatalen, and Gibson, *Elizabeth I's correspondence*, p. 29.

9. Bajetta, Coatalen, and Gibson, *Elizabeth I's correspondence*, p.

34.

10. Bajetta, Coatalen, and Gibson, *Elizabeth I's correspondence*, p. 32.

11. The Duke of Anjou to the queen, 24 Jul. 1579, *Calendar of the Cecil papers…, vol. 2,* (London, 1888), pp 261-264, British History online, https://www.british-history.ac.uk/cal-cecil-papers/vol2/pp261-264 (17 Jul. 2021).

12. Ackroyd, *Tudors*, p. 391.

13. The Duke of Anjou to the queen, 19 Aug. 1579, *Calendar of the Cecil papers…, vol. 2,* (London, 1888), pp. 264-266, British History online, https://www.british-history.ac.uk/cal-cecil-papers/vol2/pp264-266 (24 Jul. 2021).

14. Rawdon Brown and G. Cavendish Bentinck (eds.), *Calendar of state papers relating to English affairs in the archives of Venice, vol. 7, 1558-1580,* (London, 1890), Sept. 1579, pp. 611-618. British History online, http://www.british-history.ac.uk/cal-state-papers/venice/vol7/pp611-618 (24 Jul. 2020). Also see Borman, *The private lives*, p. 338.

15. Doran, *Monarchy and matrimony*, p. 255.

16. Bajetta, Coatalen, and Gibson, *Elizabeth I's correspondence*, p. 35.

17. Borman, *The private lives*, p. 338.

18. Ibid.

19. Ackroyd, *Tudors*, p. 391.

20. The Duke of Anjou to the queen, 29/30 Aug. 1579, *Calendar of the Cecil papers…, vol. 2,* (London, 1888), pp 264-266, British History online, https://www.british-history.ac.uk/cal-cecil-papers/vol2/pp264-266 (24 Jul. 2021).

21. The Duke of Anjou to the queen, 30 Aug. 1579, *Calendar of the Cecil papers…, vol. 2,* (London, 1888), pp 264-266, British History online, https://www.british-history.ac.uk/cal-cecil-papers/vol2/pp264-266 (24 Jul. 2021).

22. C. Falkus (ed.), *The private lives of the Tudor monarchs*, (London, 1974), pp 109-110.

23. Borman, *The private lives*, p. 339.
24. Levin, *The heart and stomach of a king*, p. 51.
25. Wallace T. MacCaffrey, *Queen Elizabeth and the making of policy, 1572-1588*, (Princeton, 1981), p. 254.
26. Donald Stump and Susan M. Felch, *Elizabeth and her age: a Norton critical edition*, (New York, 2009), p. 269.
27. The Duke of Anjou to the queen, 10 Oct. 1579, *Calendar of the Cecil papers...*, vol. 2, (London, 1888), pp 267-274, British History online, https://www.british-history.ac.uk/cal-cecil-papers/vol2/pp267-274 (24 Jul. 2021).
28. Neville Williams, *Elizabeth the first: queen of England*, (New York, 1968), p. 182.
29. Stump and Felch, *Elizabeth and her age*, p. 269.
30. Ibid.
31. Stump and Felch, *Elizabeth and her age*, p. 281.

Chapter 5 - A Kingdom in Opposition

1. MacCaffrey, *Queen Elizabeth*, p. 263
2. Bajetta, Coatalen, and Gibson, *Elizabeth I's correspondence*, pp. 35-36.
3. The queen's marriage, 7 Oct. 1579, 766, *Calendar of the Cecil Papers...*, Vol. 2, British History online, https://www.british-history.ac.uk/cal-cecil-papers/vol2/pp267-274, (24 Jul. 2021).
4. The Anjou marriage, 7 Oct. 1579,765, *Calendar of the Cecil Papers...*, Vol. 2, British History online, https://www.british-history.ac.uk/cal-cecil-papers/vol2/pp267-274, (24 Jul. 2021).
5. Bajetta, Coatalen, and Gibson, *Elizabeth I's correspondence*, pp. 35-36.
6. Ibid.
7. Ibid.
8. Stump and Felch, *Elizabeth and her age*, pp. 267-269.
9. Ibid.
10. Ibid.
11. Stump and Felch, *Elizabeth and her age*, pp. 277-281.

12. Ibid.
13. Ibid.
14. Ibid.
15. Ibid.
16. Ibid.
17. Ibid.
18. This Reference to Ajax and his shield is symbolic. In Homer's *Iliad,* Ajax often fought in tandem with his brother Teucer. Ajax would wield his magnificent shield, as Teucer stood behind, picking off enemy Trojans.
19. 'Stead' – meaning to help.
20. Stump and Felch, *Elizabeth and her age*, pp. 277-281.
21. Ibid.
22. Judith M. Richards, *Elizabeth I*, (Oxon, 2012), p. 112.
23. Ibid.
24. Stump and Felch, *Elizabeth and her age*, pp. 287-295.
25. Ibid.
26. Ibid.
27. Richards, *Elizabeth I*, p. 112. Also see P. L. Hughes and J. F. Larkin, *Tudor royal proclamations*, (New Haven, 1969), pp. 445-449.
28. Richards, *Elizabeth I*, p. 113.
29. Stump and Felch, *Elizabeth and her age*, pp. 266-267.
30. Ross, *The men who would be king*, p. 184.
31. Stump and Felch, *Elizabeth and her age*, pp. 266-267.
32. Stump and Felch, *Elizabeth and her age*, pp. 274-276.
33. Ibid.
34. Ibid.
35. The Duke of Anjou to the queen, 10 Oct. 1579, 767, *Calendar of the Cecil papers…, vol. 2*, (London, 1888), pp 267-274, British History online, https://www.british-history.ac.uk/cal-cecil-papers/vol2/pp267-274 (31 Jul. 2021).
36. The Duke of Anjou to the queen, 14 Nov. 1579, 769, *Calendar of the Cecil papers…, vol. 2*, (London, 1888), pp 274-280, British

History online, https://www.british-history.ac.uk/cal-cecil-papers/vol2/pp274-280 (1 Aug. 2021).

Chapter 6 - Second Chances

1. Philippa Jones, *Elizabeth: virgin queen*, (Lincolnshire, 2017), p. 218.
2. Ross, *The men who would be king*, p. 188.
3. The Duke of Anjou to the queen, 1 Dec. 1579, 778, *Calendar of the Cecil papers…, vol. 2*, (London, 1888), pp 280-303, British History online, https://www.british-history.ac.uk/cal-cecil-papers/vol2/pp280-303 (2 Aug. 2021).
4. Queen Elizabeth to the Duke of Anjou, 19 Dec. 1579, 781, *Calendar of the Cecil papers…, vol. 2*, (London, 1888), pp 280-303, British History online, https://www.british-history.ac.uk/cal-cecil-papers/vol2/pp280-303 (2 Aug. 2021).
5. G.B. Harrison (ed.), *The letters of queen Elizabeth*, (London, 1935), p. 140.
6. Pierre Clausse Seigneur de Marchaumont.
7. Jones, *Elizabeth*, p. 218.
8. Ross, *The men who would be king*, p. 186.
9. Ibid.
10. Bajetta, Coatalen, and Gibson, *Elizabeth I's correspondence*, pp. 39-40.
11. Ibid.
12. Ibid.
13. Martin Hume, *The courtships of queen Elizabeth*, (New York, 1904), pp. 211-212.
14. Jones, *Elizabeth*, p. 218.
15. Arthur John Butler (ed.) *Calendar of state papers, foreign, Elizabeth, vol. 15, 1581-1582*, pp 459-478, British History online, https://www.british-history.ac.uk/cal-state-papers/foreign/vol15/pp459-478#highlight-first (5 Jun. 2020).
16. Martin Hume (ed.), *Calendar of state papers, Spain (Simancas), vol. 3, 1580-1586*, (London, 1896), pp 219-229, British History

online, https://www.british-history.ac.uk/cal-state-papers/simancas/vol3/pp219-229, (5 Jun. 2020).

17. Stump and Felch, *Elizabeth and her age*, p. 266.

18. Borman, *The private lives*, p. 339.

19. Ibid.

20. Richards, *Elizabeth I*, p. 113.

21. Ibid.

22. Stump and Felch, *Elizabeth and her age*, pp 302-304. The original copy of Puttenham's series of poetry can be found in the British Library, (MS Cotton Vespasian E. VII, fols. 172r-173r.

23. Ibid.

24. Ibid.

25. Harrison, *The letters of queen Elizabeth*, p. 129.

26. Bell, 'Elizabeth I and the policy of marriage', p. 86.

27. Ross, *The men who would be king*, p. 189.

28. Ibid.

29. Ross, *The men who would be king*, pp. 192-195.

30. Ibid.

31. Ibid.

32. Hume, *Calendar of state papers, Spain,* p. 226.

33. Helen Castor, *Elizabeth I: 1558-1603*, (London, 2018), pp. 67-68.

34. Ibid.

35. Ibid.

36. Ibid.

37. Ibid.

38. Guy, *Elizabeth*, p. 34.

39. Ibid.

Chapter 7 - The Question of Succession

1. Borman, *The private lives*, p. 272.

2. Ibid.

3. King, 'Queen Elizabeth I', pp. 30-31.

4. Stump and Felch, *Elizabeth and her age*, pp. 77-79.
5. Ibid.
6. Stump and Felch, *Elizabeth and her age*, p. 123.
7. Borman, *The private lives*, p. 281.
8. Stump and Felch, *Elizabeth and her age*, p. 141.
9. Stump and Felch, *Elizabeth and her age*, p. 137.
10. Stump and Felch, *Elizabeth and her age*, p. 138.
11. Stump and Felch, *Elizabeth and her age*, pp. 140-141.
12. Borman, *The private lives*, p. 279.
13. Brown and Cavendish Bentinck, *Calendar of state papers… Venice*, p. 601.
14. Jones, *Elizabeth*, p. 65.
15. Jones, *Elizabeth*, p. 67.
16. Princess Elizabeth to dowager queen Katherine Parr, c. Jun. 1548, (The National Archives, SP10/2 f. 84c).
17. Ross, *The men who would be king*, p. 194.
18. Richards, *Elizabeth I*, pp. 68-69.
19. Richards, *Elizabeth I*, p. 21.
20. Richards, *Elizabeth I*, p. 68.
21. Marcus, Mueller, and Rose, *Elizabeth I: collected works*, pp. 120-125.

Chapter 8 - On Monsieur's Departure

1. Hilton, *Elizabeth*, pp. 239-240.
2. Guy, *Elizabeth*, p. 48.
3. Hilton, *Elizabeth*, pp. 239-240.
4. Jones, *Elizabeth*, p. 219.
5. Ross, *The men who would be king*, pp. 198-199.
6. Ibid.
7. Hilton, *Elizabeth*, p. 240.
8. Stump and Felch, *Elizabeth and her age*, p. 268.
9. Ross, *The men who would be king*, pp. 198-199.
10. Ibid.
11. Hilton, *Elizabeth*, p. 240.

12. Ross, *The men who would be king*, pp. 198-199.
13. Marcus, Mueller, and Rose, *Elizabeth I: collected works*, pp 302-303.
14. Borman, *The private lives*, p. 339.
15. Ross, *The men who would be king*, pp. 198-199.
16. Castor, *Elizabeth I*, p. 69.
17. Mears, 'Love making and diplomacy', pp. 454-455.
18. Ibid.
19. Hammer, 'Sex and the virgin queen', p. 81.

Chapter 9 - The Extremity of My Misfortune

1-14. Marcus, Mueller, and Rose, *Elizabeth I: collected works*, pp. 253-256
15. Jones, *Elizabeth*, p. 220. Also see Borman, *The private lives*, p. 339 and Anniina Jokinen, 'Biography of François, duke of Alençon and Anjou', Luminarium Encyclopedia online, http://www.luminarium.org/encyclopedia/alencon.htm, (25 Jun. 2020).
16. Ibid.
17. Borman, *The private lives*, p. 340.
18-23. Marcus, Mueller, and Rose, *Elizabeth I: collected works*, pp. 260-261.
24. Ross, *The men who would be king*, p. 200.
25. Marcus, Mueller, and Rose, *Elizabeth I: collected works*, pp. 303-304.

Chapter 10 - All My Husbands.

1. King, 'Queen Elizabeth I', p. 30.
2. Ross, *The men who would be king*, p. 202.
3. Christopher Haigh, *Elizabeth I*, (Harlow, 2000), p. 24.
4. Ross, *The men who would be king*, p. 202.
5. Jones, *Elizabeth*, p. 220.
6. Ross, *The men who would be king*, p. 204
7. Ibid

8. Ibid.
9. Ibid.
10. Ross, *The men who would be king*, p. 205.
11. Stump and Felch, *Elizabeth and her age*, p. 435.
12. Ibid.
13. Ibid.
14. I Stump and Felch, *Elizabeth and her age*, p. 436.
15. Castor, *Elizabeth I*, pp. 94-95.
16. Ibid.
17. Castor, *Elizabeth I*, p. 96.
18. Hilton, *Elizabeth*, p. 322.
19. F.H. Mares (ed.), *The memoirs of Robert Carey*, (Oxford, 1972), p. 59.

Bibliography

Note: The existing literature based on Elizabeth I and her courtships is vast. The primary and secondary sources that I have consulted are from personal selection and are by no means the only existing sources in relation to Elizabeth's courtship to the Duke of Anjou. The select secondary sources I have chosen mostly come from authors and historians that I trust and regard highly for their ability, discipline, interpretation and passion. These particular sources represent the ongoing debate regarding this book's topic(s).

Calendar of State Papers (online printed versions)

Calendar of the Cecil papers in Hatfield House: Volume 1, 1306-1571 (London, 1883), British History online, https://www.british-history.ac.uk/cal-cecil-papers/vol1.

Calendar of the Cecil papers in Hatfield House: Volume 2, 1572-1582 (London, 1888), British History online, http://www.british-history.ac.uk/cal-cecil-papers/vol2.

Calendar of the Cecil papers in Hatfield House: Volume 3, 1583-1589 (London, 1889), British History online, https://www.british-history.ac.uk/cal-cecil-papers/vol3.

Calendar of state papers foreign: Elizabeth, Volume 1, 1558-1559, Joseph Stevenson (ed.) (London, 1863), British History online, https://www.british-history.ac.uk/cal-state-papers/foreign/vol1.

Calendar of state papers, foreign, Elizabeth, Volume 15, 1581-1582, Arthur John Butler (ed.) (London, 1907) British History online, https://www.british-history.ac.uk/cal-state-papers/foreign/vol15.

Calendar of state papers, Spain (Simancas), Volume 1, 1558-1567, Martin Hume (ed.) (London, 1892), pp 219-229, British History online, https://www.british-history.ac.uk/cal-state-papers/simancas/vol1.

Calendar of state papers, Spain (Simancas), Volume 2, 1568-1579, Martin Hume (ed.) (London, 1894), British History online, https://www.british-history.ac.uk/cal-state-papers/simancas/vol2.

Calendar of state papers, Spain (Simancas), Volume 3, 1580-1586, Martin Hume (ed.) (London, 1896), British History online, https://www.british-history.ac.uk/cal-state-papers/simancas/vol3.

Calendar of state papers relating to English affairs in the archives of Venice, vol. 7, 1558-1580, Rawdon Brown and G. Cavendish Bentinck (eds.) (London, 1890), British History online, https://www.british-history.ac.uk/cal-state-papers/venice/vol7.

Primary Sources (Archival)

Calendar of state papers, foreign, general series, Elizabeth I, letters and papers, June-July 1559 (NA Kew, SP 70/5, fos. 183-184).

Hardwicke State Papers, I, British Library London, MS 25830, fos. 158-9.

Princess Elizabeth to Dowager Queen Katherine Parr, c. June 1548, The National Archives, (SP10/2 f.84c).

'The Lady Elizabeth's answer made at Hatfield to Sir Thomas Pope' 26 April, 1558, BL Harleian MS 444, fols. 20-9.

Printed Primary Sources

Bajetta, Carlo M, Coatalen, Guillaume, and Gibson, Jonathan, (eds.), *Elizabeth I's correspondence: letters, rhetoric and politics,* (New York, 2014).

Berry, Lloyd E., (ed.), *John Stubbs's 'Gaping Gulf' with letters and other relevant documents,* (Charlottesville, 1968).

Camden, W., *The history of the most renowned and victorious princess Elizabeth, late queen of England,* (London, 1675).

Harrison, G.B, (ed.), *The letters of queen Elizabeth* I, (London,1935).

Hartley, T.E, *Proceedings in the parliaments of Elizabeth, 1585-1589,*

Volume 2, (Leicester, 1995).

Marcus, Leah S., Mueller, Janel, and Rose, Mary Beth, (eds.), *Elizabeth I: collected works,* (Chicago, 2002).

Mares, F.H., (ed.), *The memoirs of Robert Carey,* (Oxford, 1972).

May, Steven W., *Queen Elizabeth I: selected works,* (New York, 2004).

Murdin, W., (ed.), *A collection of state papers relating to affairs in the reign of queen Elizabeth from the year 1571 to 1576,* (London, 1759).

Peck, D.C, (ed.) *Leicester's commonwealth: copy of a letter written by a master of Cambridge (1584) and related documents,* (Athens, 1985).

Stump, Donald and Felch, Susan M., *Elizabeth and her age: a Norton critical edition,* (New York, 2009).

Thickett, Dorothy, *Etienne pasquier: lettres historiques pour les années 1556-1594,* (Geneva, 1966).

Primary Sources (digitized)

Aylmer, J. *An harborowe for faithful and trewe subiects,* (London, 1559), sigs. B2v, G3, H3v, online, https://lib.ugent.be/en/catalog/rug01:001502047.

Coroner's report into the death of Amy Robsart, August 1561 (KB 9/1073/f.80), National Archives online https://www.nationalarchives.gov.uk/education/resources/elizabeth-monarchy/coroners-report/.

Elizabeth I to King Eric XIV of Sweden, 25 February 1560 (SP 70/11 f.74), National Archives History online, https://www.nationalarchives.gov.uk/education/resources/elizabeth-monarchy/elizabeth-i-to-king-eric-xiv-of-sweden/.

Secondary sources (books)

Ackroyd, Peter, *Tudors: the history of England,* (London, 2012).

Adams, Simon, Bernard, G. W., (eds.), *Religion, politics, and society in sixteenth-century England,* (Cambridge, 2003).

Borman, Tracey, *The private lives of the Tudors: uncovering the secrets of Britain's greatest dynasty,* (London, 2016).

Castor, Helen, *Elizabeth I: 1558-1603,* (London, 2018).

De Lisle, Leanda, *Tudor: the family story,* (London, 2013).

Doran Susan, *Elizabeth I and her circle,* (Oxford, 2015).

Doran, Susan, Monarchy *and matrimony: the courtships of Elizabeth I,* (London, 1996).

Falkus, C., (ed.), *The private lives of the Tudor monarchs,* (London, 1974).

Guy, John *Elizabeth: The forgotten years,* (London, 2016).

Haigh, Christopher, *Elizabeth I,* (Harlow, 2000).

Hibbert, C, *Elizabeth I: a personal history of the virgin queen,* (London, 1992).

Hilton, Lisa, *Elizabeth: renaissance prince, a biography,* (London, 2014).

Holt, Mack P., *The duke of Anjou and the politique struggle during the wars of religion,* (Cambridge, 1986).

Hughes P.L, and Larkin, J.F, *Tudor royal proclamations,* (New Haven, 1969).

Hume, Martin, *The courtships of queen Elizabeth,* (New York, 1904).

Jenkins, Elizabeth, *Elizabeth the great,* (New York, 1958).

Jones, Norman, *The birth of the Elizabethan age: England in the 1560s: a history of early modern England,* (Cambridge,1993).

Jones, Philippa, *Elizabeth: virgin queen,* (Lincolnshire, 2017).

Knecht, Robert J., *The French religious wars 1562-98*, (Harlow, 2000).

Levin, Carole, *The heart and stomach of a king: Elizabeth I and the politics of sex and power,* (Philadelphia, 2013).

Loades, David, *Elizabeth I,* (London, 2003).

Loades, David, *Mary Tudor: a life,* (Oxford, 1989).

MacCaffrey, Wallace T., *Queen Elizabeth and the making of policy, 1572-88,* (Princeton, 1981).

Richards, Judith M., *Elizabeth I,* (Oxon, 2012).

Porter, Linda, *Katherine the queen: the remarkable life of Katherine*

Parr, (London, 2010).

Ross, Josephine, *The men who would be king: the courtships of queen Elizabeth I,* (New York, 1975).

Somerset, Anne, *Ladies in waiting: from the Tudors to the present day,* (London, 2005).

Strong, Roy, *Gloriana: the portraits of queen Elizabeth I,* (London,1987).

Tallis, Nicola, *Elizabeth's rival: the tumultuous tale of Lettice Knollys, countess of Leicester,* (London, 2017).

Weir, Alison, *The life of Elizabeth,* (New York, 1998).

Whitelock, Anna, *Mary Tudor: England's first queen,* (London, 2009).

Williams, Penry, *The later Tudors: England 1547-1603,* (Oxford, 1995).

Williams, Neville, *Elizabeth the first: queen of England,* (New York,1968).

Journal articles

Hammer, Paul E. J., 'Sex and the virgin queen: aristocratic concupiscence and the court of Elizabeth I', in *The Sixteenth Century Journal,* vol. 31, no. 1 (2000), pp. 77-97.

Heydt, Bruce, 'Amy Robsart's revenge?' in *British Heritage,* vol. 25, issue 1 (2004), pp. 28-33.

Holt, Mack P., 'Patterns of clientèle and economic opportunity at court during the wars of religion: the household of François, duke of Anjou' in *French Historical Studies,* vol. 13, no. 3 (1984), pp. 305-322.

King, John N., 'Queen Elizabeth I: representations of the virgin queen' in *Renaissance Quarterly,* vol. 43, no. 1, (1990), pp. 30-74.

Mears, Natalie, 'Love making and diplomacy: Elizabeth I and the Anjou marriage negotiations, c. 1578 – 1582', in *The Historical Association,* (2001), pp. 442-466.

Online secondary sources

Jokinen, Anniina. 'Biography of François, duke of Alençon and Anjou' in *Luminarium Encyclopaedia*, (2008), online, http://www.luminarium.org/encyclopedia/alencon.htm.

Prince Hercule François, Duc d'Alençon 1572, oil on canvas, 189 x 102 cm, National Gallery of Art, Washington D.C. online, https://www.wga.hu/html_m/m/master/yunk_fr/yunk_fr1/124princ.html.

Bell, Aryn Elizabeth, 'Elizabeth I and the policy of marriage: the Anjou match, 1572-1582', (2013), Theses and dissertations, 1397. https://commons.und.edu/theses/1397.

Recent bestsellers from Chronos Books are:

Lady Katherine Knollys
The Unacknowledged Daughter of King Henry VIII
Sarah-Beth Watkins
A comprehensive account of Katherine Knollys' questionable
paternity, her previously unexplored life in the Tudor court
and her intriguing relationship with Elizabeth I.
Paperback: 978-1-78279-585-8 ebook: 978-1-78279-584-1

Cromwell was Framed
Ireland 1649
Tom Reilly
Revealed: The definitive research that proves the Irish nation
owes Oliver Cromwell a huge posthumous apology for
wrongly convicting him of civilian atrocities in 1649.
Paperback: 978-1-78279-516-2 ebook: 978-1-78279-515-5

Why The CIA Killed JFK and Malcolm X
The Secret Drug Trade in Laos
John Koerner
A new groundbreaking work presenting evidence that the CIA
silenced JFK to protect its secret drug trade in Laos.
Paperback: 978-1-78279-701-2 ebook: 978-1-78279-700-5

The Disappearing Ninth Legion
A Popular History
Mark Olly
The Disappearing Ninth Legion examines hard evidence for the
foundation, development, mysterious disappearance, or possi-
ble continuation of Rome's lost Legion.
Paperback: 978-1-84694-559-5 ebook: 978-1-84694-931-9

Beaten But Not Defeated
Siegfried Moos - A German anti-Nazi who settled in Britain
Merilyn Moos
Siegi Moos, an anti-Nazi and active member of the German
Communist Party, escaped Germany in 1933 and, exiled in
Britain, sought another route to the transformation
of capitalism.
Paperback: 978-1-78279-677-0 ebook: 978-1-78279-676-3

A Schoolboy's Wartime Letters
An evacuee's life in WWII — A Personal Memoir
Geoffrey Iley
A boy writes home during WWII, revealing his own fascinating
story, full of zest for life, information and humour.
Paperback: 978-1-78279-504-9 ebook: 978-1-78279-503-2

The Life & Times of the Real Robyn Hoode
Mark Olly
A journey of discovery. The chronicles of the genuine historical
character, Robyn Hoode, and how he became one of England's
greatest legends.
Paperback: 978-1-78535-059-7 ebook: 978-1-78535-060-3